L WELFARE IN CHINA

POLICY IN CONTEMPORARY CHINA
n)

Business, Government and Society

ENT (*third edition*)

MENT IN EUROPE (*co-editor with Franz Strehl*)

The Market in Chinese Social Policy

Edited by

Linda Wong

and

Norman Flynn

First published 2001 by
PALGRAVE
Houndmills, Basingstoke, Hampshire RG21 6XS and
175 Fifth Avenue, New York, N. Y. 10010
Companies and representatives throughout the world

PALGRAVE is the new global academic imprint of
St. Martin's Press LLC Scholarly and Reference Division and
Palgrave Publishers Ltd (formerly Macmillan Press Ltd).

ISBN 0–333–91779–0

This book is printed on paper suitable for recycling and
made from fully managed and sustained forest sources.

A catalogue record for this book is available
from the British Library.

Library of Congress Cataloging-in-Publication Data
The market in Chinese social policy / edited by Linda Wong
and Norman Flynn.
        p. cm.
    Includes bibliographical references and index.
    ISBN 0–333–91779–0 (cloth)
    1. China—Social policy. 2. China—Economic policy—1976–
3. China—Economic conditions—1976– I. Wong, Linda, 1949–
II. Flynn, Norman.
    HN733.5 .M363 2001
    361.6'1'0951—dc21
                                              00–054205

10 9   8   7   6   5   4   3   2   1
10 09 08 07 06 05 04 03 02 01

Printed and bound in Great Britain by
Antony Rowe Ltd, Chippenham, Wiltshire

Contents

List of Tables and Figures

Tables

Figures

Acknowledgements

The book grew out of the constant dialogue and debates among teachers in one university department who share interests in the role of marketization and privatization in social life. Our interests in developments in China have grown over the course of teaching and research at the City University of Hong Kong, hence the idea of a book that provides the forum for each to test out ideas on market inroads into various social policies in China in the era of economic reform drew instant support. To guide us in our common pursuit, two workshops were held. We also invited Bob Deacon to share insights drawn from social policy reforms in Eastern Europe and elsewhere. In the final stage of revising the manuscript, three colleagues – Adrian Sinfield, Zsuzsa Ferge and Ian Holliday – offered many useful comments. Ian also took part in co-writing the introduction and conclusion. The hard work of all contributors is much appreciated.

Funds for research and the two workshops came from the Contemporary China Research Centre of City University. Without this grant, the current enterprise would have been impossible.

Last but not least, we would like to thank Huen Wai-po and Lisa Wong for helping to prepare the country profile and the typescript.

LINDA WONG

Notes on the Contributors

Anthony B.L. Cheung is Head and Associate Professor, Department of Public and Social Administration at the City University of Hong Kong. An ex-civil servant and a specialist in public administration, he has published books and articles on privatization, civil service and public sector reforms, and government and politics in Hong Kong and China. His recent books are *Public Sector Reform in Hong Kong* (co-edited with Jane Lee, 1995) and *The Civil Service in Hong Kong: Continuity and Change* (co-authored with Shafiqul Huque and Grace O.M. Lee, 1998).

Bob Deacon is Professor of Social Policy at the University of Sheffield and Director of the Globalism and Social Policy Programme (GASPP) which is based partly at Sheffield and partly at STAKES (National Research Centre for Welfare and Health), Helsinki, Finland. He is the author of several books on East European and post-Communist social policy. The most recent is *Global Social Policy*. He is founding editor of a new journal, *Global Social Policy*, which is an inter-disciplinary journal of public policy and social development. He has also acted as consultant to several international organizations including the United Nations Development Programme (UNDP), Human Development Report, International Labour Organization (ILO), European Union (EU), Council of Europe and United Nations Research Institute in Social Development (UNRISD).

Norman Flynn currently runs the Public Services Management Programme at the London School of Economics. Previously he has been Professor of Public Sector Management at the City University of Hong Kong and lecturer at Birmingham University and London Business School. He has written about public policy and management issues in the UK and Europe and about business, government and society in East and South-east Asia. His books include *Miracle to Meltdown: Business, Government and Society* (1999), *Public Sector Management* (3rd edn 1997), and *Public Sector Management in Europe* (ed. with Franz Strehl, 1996).

Ian Holliday is Professor of Policy Studies, Department of Public and Social Administration, City University of Hong Kong. Previously he taught at the University of Manchester and at New York University. His research interests include comparative social policy, with a focus on healthcare, and comparative institutional analysis, with a focus on core executives. His books include *The British Cabinet System* (with Martin Burch, 1996) and *The NHS Transformed* (2nd edn 1995). He co-edits the journal *Party Politics*.

K.Y. Lau is Associate Professor, Department of Public and Social Administration, City University of Hong Kong. His research and publications focus on housing policy and administration in Hong Kong and urban housing system reform in China. He is a member of the Hong Kong Housing Authority and served as a member of the Hong Kong Government Housing Bureau Long Term Housing Strategy Review Steering Group between 1996 and 1998.

Grace O.M. Lee is Assistant Professor, Department of Public and Social Administration, City University of Hong Kong. She was an officer with the Labour Department of the Hong Kong Government before joining the academic profession. Her research interests include labour studies and public sector management. She has published extensively on labour issues in Hong Kong and China, and public management in the Hong Kong civil service. She is the co-author (with Anthony B.L. Cheung and Shafiqul Huque) of *The Civil Service in Hong Kong: Continuity and Change* (1998).

James Lee is Associate Professor, Department of Public and Social Administration, City University of Hong Kong. He specializes in housing studies and housing policy, with an emphasis on home ownership, housing management and comparative housing policy. His current research projects include housing affordability in Hong Kong and comparative housing studies of Hong Kong and Shanghai. His books include *The New Social Policy* (co-edited with Kam-wah Chan, Lai-ching Leung and Sammy Chiu, 1999) and *Housing, Home Ownership and Social Change in Hong Kong* (2000).

Ka-ho Mok is Convenor of the Comparative Education Policy Research Unit in the Department of Public and Social Administration at the City University of Hong Kong. He is also Associate Professor in the same department. His major research interests include comparative education policy, social and political development issues in contemporary China, and intellectuals and politics. He is the author of *Intellectuals and the State in Post-Mao China* (1998) and *Social and Political Development in Post-Reform China* (2000). He has also published articles in *Comparative Education Review, International Review of Education, Comparative Education* and *Higher Education*.

Linda Wong is Associate Professor, Department of Public and Social Administration, at the City University of Hong Kong. She has published books and articles on various social development issues in China, including social welfare, unemployment, social welfare development in the Pearl River Delta, and migration policy. She is the author of *Social Welfare under Chinese Socialism: Study on Civil Affairs Welfare* (in Chinese, 1995) and *Marginalization and Social Welfare in China* (1998), and co-editor (with Stewart MacPherson) of *Social Change and Social Policy in Contemporary China* (1995).

List of Abbreviations

AIA	American International Assurance Company
CCF	China Charity Federation
CCP	Chinese Communist Party
CLSY	*China Labour Statistical Yearbook*
COEs	collective-owned enterprises
HPF	Housing Provident Fund
ILO	International Labour Organization
IMF	International Monetary Fund
MCA	Ministry of Civil Affairs
MLSS	Ministry of Labour and Social Security
NGOs	non-governmental organizations
SEC	State Education Commission
SEZ	Special Economic Zone
SOEs	state-owned enterprises
SSB	State Statistical Bureau
TVEs	township and village enterprises
UNDP	United Nations Development Programme
UNFPA	United Nations Population Fund
UNICEF	United Nations Children's Fund
WHO	World Health Organization
WTO	World Trade Organization

1
Introduction

Norman Flynn, Ian Holliday and Linda Wong

Embracing the market

Fascination with markets has been a global phenomenon in recent decades. The application of market principles to public-sector organizations and operations, and the resultant impact of market and quasi-market forces on state activities, have been pervasive as well as profound. In macro-economic management, public service provision, social programme delivery, policy formulation and governance, market values and practices have made significant inroads. In the 1980s Reagan and Thatcher were no doubt the most notable advocates of market-based approaches, but since then American and British ways of restructuring and managing the public sector and public finances have been followed by developed and developing countries alike. The collapse of Communism in the former Soviet Union and East-Central Europe added new converts to the cause as market principles were embraced with differing degrees of enthusiasm both within and between states. Even in the bloc of countries that continued to profess a commitment to socialism, attempts were made to shift from plan to market. Among those states, none has gained a higher profile than China for the thorough manner in which markets have been developed on most fronts.

The success of China's economic reforms in the 1990s captured the attention of much of the world, not least because it stood in stark contrast to the economic collapse witnessed in the former Soviet Union. Whereas Russia and much of East-Central Europe made only faltering steps towards a market economy, China was able to point to a dynamic indigenous private sector and significant inward investment, notably in the coastal regions of the south and east. China also registered consistently high rates of economic progress that suggested it might follow other East Asian states (such as Japan) and the four tiger economies of Hong Kong, Singapore, South Korea and Taiwan down the growth path. In universities and transnational agencies such as the International Monetary Fund (IMF) and the World Bank, economists, political scientists and others sought to determine the reasons for these distinct experiences. They focused particularly on the more incremental and gradualist course taken by reform in China, and on the considerable political control imposed on the process of economic transformation by the Chinese Communist Party (CCP).

Our concerns in this volume are different. The focus of interest is not economic reform in and of itself, but the impact a shift to market principles in very many spheres of Chinese public life has had on the critical sector of social policy. In many ways social policy reform has been driven by economic transformation, as profound structural change has had inevitable knock-on effects in the social policy domain. Moreover, to many key policy makers it has seemed logical that social sectors should be adapted to marketized modes of operation, so that the economic and social spheres retain a high degree of compatibility. But behind the generalized embrace of the market lies a series of complex and diverse processes of social policy change. The aim of this volume is to explore those processes as a means of understanding the ways in which marketization has been played out in distinct social policy sectors.

Social policy in China

It need hardly be said that social policy reform in China is a huge topic. China is in no sense a routine social, economic and political entity. It is effectively a continental polity, and at the end of 1997 had a population of 1 236 000 000. Each of the country's 31 provinces is itself a sizeable social, economic and political system. The large provinces to the west and north of the country are considerably bigger than any West European state. Provinces such as Sichuan in the southern centre and Shandong on the eastern seaboard, with respective populations of 112 and 87 million, are more populous than any such state. The differences between, say, the fast-growing cities of the coastal region in the south and east and the rural areas of much of the north and west are great enough to make these effectively different worlds (Goodman, 1997).

That said, there are some general aspects of Chinese social policy that can be sketched at the outset to provide a context for the rest of this study. Not long after the socialist transformation of the mid-1950s,

Chinese citizens came under the protective embrace of a paternalistic state as the fabled 'iron rice-bowl' was gradually made the centrepiece of Communist social policy. Whilst it was certainly pervasive, this was never a uniform system of social protection. In towns and cities, a state-assigned job effectively became the birthright of registered dwellers. Once assigned, workers were enveloped in a relationship with the state-owned employer that combined employment protection with a range of welfare services including housing, health, education and pension rights. The expectation was that the individual would stay with one work unit either for a long time or, frequently, for life. In time positions even began to be passed down the generations. In China's vast rural hinterland peasants were engaged in work at the collective farm. Rural communes and production brigades furnished the basis for provision of life support and social services such as schools, clinics and assistance for the indigent. As far as living standards were concerned, life in the countryside was far tougher than in urban areas. Yet moving to the cities was impossible, because of the household registration regulation implemented in 1958.

One central feature of this social policy system was that it operated through the employment contract. It was through state-owned enterprises (SOEs) and collective-owned enterprises (COEs) in urban areas, and through communes in rural areas, that the state conducted the main bulk of its social policy. All sorts of costs came with this system, including highly intrusive state direction of labour. But there were benefits too in the comprehensive social protection offered to many Chinese people. In towns and cities in particular, the Chinese welfare system performed to a high standard. Indeed, China was singled out by a leading comparative study as 'one of the star performers among the low-income nations in meeting basic needs', though its poor human rights record was simultaneously criticized (Doyal and Gough, 1991, p.270).

In all the turmoil experienced by China in the Maoist period, including the Great Leap Forward of the late 1950s and the Cultural Revolution of the late 1960s, the cosy system of social protection under paternalistic socialism remained largely untouched. Only with the death of Mao in 1976 and the political ascendancy of Deng later in the decade did real reform begin to take place. The key event was the Third Plenum of the Chinese Communist Party's Central Committee, held in 1978, which introduced a comprehensive programme of economic reform. That programme was not uncontested, for although in the post-Mao period many elite Party officials agreed that change was needed, there was no consensus about what should be changed or how change should be managed. Factions in favour of rapid moves towards market mechanisms ('marketeers') confronted those who were more cautious ('adjusters') (Meisner, 1996, p.209). One consequence was that in the two decades since 1978 there have been periods of 'loosening' and 'tightening' as distinct factions have gained and lost influence (Lieberthal, 1995). Nevertheless, the Third Plenum in 1978 turned out to be the critical point in the process that has seen a series of fundamental reforms sweep China. Although those reforms were initially economic, they necessarily had immediate social policy consequences because of the major transformation of structural relations brought about by economic revolution.

Change came first in the countryside, where the system of collective farms that had formed the core of agricultural organization was slowly deconstructed. The most notable reform was introduction of a household responsibility system, which was critical in undermining the collective framework. Other new agrarian policies were also pursued, including abolition of the state monopoly on grain purchase, introduction of market prices for farm produce, and development of rural industry. Alongside these changes in agricultural organization were a series of institutional reforms. A new constitution promulgated in 1982 provided for the abolition of communes, and from 1983 onwards their administrative functions were transferred to township (*zhen*) or village (*xiang*) councils. From 1984 a loosening in the registration system allowed peasants to move into towns and cities for work and business without changing their rural status on condition that they took responsibility for arranging their own food grain, capital and housing (Solinger, 1991). One key element of China's economic miracle has been the development of township and village enterprises (TVEs), which have fostered growth and prosperity across much of rural China.

The institutional changes that followed the shift away from collective farms have had significant impacts on social policy. In particular, the abolition of communes raised an immediate problem of welfare funding. Under the pre-reform system, finance for collective health, education and welfare projects came from the commune welfare fund, with money deducted from collective income before being allocated to households. When agriculture was de-collectivized, money had to be scraped together from various sources, such as taxes, profits from rural enterprises (if any) and household levies after primary distribution (Hussain, 1989). In many instances peasant resistance to levies meant there was a shortage of funds for communal welfare.

In a number of sectors one consequence was often the disintegration of welfare mechanisms. Cooperative medical schemes, which were highly effective in ensuring peasant access to healthcare in the pre-reform period, largely collapsed once reform set in (Taylor, 1988; Henderson, 1990; Pearson, 1995). Today, medical care in most villages operates on market principles. With fee for service the norm, many peasants find it hard to afford treatment. Preventive care has also suffered from neglect, with the result that in some regions communicable and infectious diseases have re-emerged. At the same time, valuable human resources, such as doctors and teachers, have been lost as individuals have responded to the government's call to get rich by changing to more lucrative occupations (Davis, 1989). For much the same reason, school enrolments have fallen as parents have withdrawn their children to work in family farms and village enterprises. Not unexpectedly, most of the dropouts have been girls. All these problems have been more severe in some regions than in others. With social funding entirely dependent on local budgets, poor rural areas have suffered the most. Meanwhile, suburban districts around big cities with good transport and better resources are sometimes able to afford improved social amenities. More inequality thus pervades contemporary social development in China.

Change in urban areas was the second stage of reform. When China had a command economy, all enterprises came under the ownership of either the state or the collective. Attached to different tiers of government, subordinate units were run by bureaucratic fiat, which meant that decisions relating to capital, labour, raw materials, output and sales were made by higher authorities. As the command economy was curtailed, so market prices began to apply to all but a limited number of selected materials and products. The development of a market economy had a major impact on nationalized industries, which were forced to respond to market signals in planning production. They were also faced with an emergent non-state sector, financed by both domestic and international capital, which quickly gained a competitive edge over the old nationalized sector. Slowly, a more diversified ownership pattern took shape. In 1978, around 80 per cent of the urban workforce were employed by SOEs and 20 per cent by COEs. By 1996, 64 per cent worked for SOEs and 17 per cent for COEs. The domestic private sector now employed 13 per cent, and the foreign and joint-ownership sector 6 per cent (*Zhongguo Tongji Nianjian* 1997, p.93).

In towns and cities reform of the labour system has had major consequences for social policy. The move to enhance enterprise incentives was accompanied by wider use of piece rates and performance-based wages. Especially important were four labour regulations that came into effect in October 1986. The 'Temporary Regulations on the Implementation of Labour Contracts in State-owned Enterprises' abolished life tenure for new recruits into state enterprises. By the end of 1996, the number of contract employees stood at 76 million, or 51 per cent of all urban workers (*Zhongguo Tongji Nianjian* 1997, p.93). Ultimately, the intention is to turn even tenured workers into contract staff. The 'Temporary Regulations on the Recruitment of Workers in State-owned Enterprises' made possible open recruitment and competitive examinations for posts. It also abrogated the system of *ding ti* which provided the option of substituting an adult child for a parent who left a work unit (Davis, 1988). The effect of the 'Temporary Regulations on the Dismissal of Workers in State-owned Enterprises Who Have Violated Discipline' was to give firms the right to fire employees who repeatedly disobey orders. Grounds for dismissal include 'having a poor attitude to service' and 'quarrelling with customers'. Finally, the 'Temporary Regulations on Unemployment Insurance for Workers in State-owned Enterprises' legalized unemployment insurance, hitherto anathema to a socialist state. During a period of redundancy, an allowance equivalent to 50–75 per cent of the workers' basic wage (revised in 1993 to 120–150 per cent of the local social relief rate) can be paid, for up to a maximum of two years. Behind each of these reforms is official alarm over escalating social security costs. Moreover, in the pre-reform system administration and funding were borne almost entirely by work units, as were welfare amenities and housing for employees. Such social obligations became a big burden. If enterprises were to become truly competitive, they had to reduce their employee responsibilities. A free flow of labour would not be possible if welfare services and social security were still tied to the work unit (see Chapter 2).

As economic reform has spread across China, so economic and social life has been altered to an unprecedented extent. In social care, new providers have emerged. Neighbourhood agencies have become more active in running services such as clinics, childcare facilities, homes for the aged, provision for the disabled, and special schools. Another channel of provision is voluntary organizations. In a more tolerant ideological climate, voluntary agencies of many kinds – local non-governmental organizations (NGOs), domestic charities, religious groups, international agencies – have begun to offer a range of social provision banned since the early 1950s. Their services include schools, clinics, rural development projects, childcare facilities, rehabilitation services and programmes for the elderly. The impact made by these bodies remains limited at present, but can only increase in the future. Other new suppliers operate in the market. Private schools, nurseries, hospitals and nursing homes have quietly emerged. Though still in their infancy, commercial services are also likely to develop, especially if economic growth continues and generates the resources needed to underpin a thriving private sector (see Chapter 3).

In the broad field of welfare provision the diversity of organizational forms that is now emerging is perhaps the most striking feature of the current reforms. While some institutions, including welfare agencies, hospitals and universities, are directly managed by ministries and other state organs, there is by no means a monolithic structure of hierarchical management. In the provision of welfare and relief programmes, the role of state agencies as financier and provider is matched, and perhaps even surpassed, by community organizations. Many NGOs, both local and overseas, have also joined the field (see Chapter 3). In healthcare, rural provision now operates mostly on a fee-for-service basis, although ownership remains public. To liberalize management and increase sources of funding, a series of experiments has taken place in many cities, notably Jiujiang and Zhenjiang, which have spearheaded reformed health insurance schemes funded by employer and employee contributions with elements comprising individual accounts, out-of-pocket expenditures and community risk-pooling (see Chapter 4). In education transfers of responsibility have usually shifted control from a state institution to another form of collective ownership and provision. *Minban*, or community-run schools, which were a common part of the pre-reform education system and were promoted during the Cultural Revolution, have been revived as a means of reducing the burden on the state for financing and managing education. A modified form of *minban*, the *minban gongzhu* school, is community-run but state-funded, allowing devolution of responsibility while maintaining some state funding. Particularly at the more expensive end of the education market, privately owned for-profit schools have emerged (see Chapter 5). In housing, policy is explicitly designed to create a mixture of for-profit, non-profit and (eventually) non-subsidized state sectors. The sale of public housing to individual tenants represents a simple transfer from public (workplace or municipality) to individual ownership, though sometimes restrictions remain on what individuals can do with their property once they own it. In the housing sector as a whole the growth of the luxury private sector represents a transformation of housing from a state benefit allocated according to some criterion of need to a simple market commodity. The provision of cost-price 'comfortable living housing' represents a middle type of provision for working urban residents (see Chapter 6).

The rise of the market in Chinese social policy

The theme that is common to change in all Chinese social policy sectors is an embracing of the market. One of the central aims of this volume is to explore the extent of particularity and difference in distinct policy sectors. It is precisely because there is a need to move away from excessive generalization that the chapters which follow have been written. However, as a means of providing some overall context for the detailed sectoral analyses in this book, the main trends in the rise of the market in Chinese social policy are briefly surveyed here.

In some spheres the production of social services by the state has been restructured with the explicit intention of meeting the perceived needs of consumers and the market. The impact of this kind of reform has been felt in the type, quantity and quality of social policy output produced by the Chinese public sector. An example is the tertiary education system, which has been substantially reshaped to meet the perceived manpower requirements of a high-tech service economy. Now that market forces predominate in curriculum planning, courses such as business administration, accountancy, computer science, law and engineering proliferate in Chinese universities. At the same time, subjects in the arts, humanities and social sciences have suffered cutbacks as a result of declining enrolment (see Chapter 5).

Another form of market incursion is increased competition between suppliers. This usually involves encouraging multiple providers to establish themselves alongside state agencies as an alternative source of social protection. The new providers that have developed in China include NGOs, independent agencies, community groups, commercial operators and volunteers. These providers have multiple relationships with the remaining state agencies. In some instances the competition is direct. In others it is virtually non-existent as social policy becomes increasingly fragmented and compartmentalized. In still others a complex set of interactions may be seen, as the kinds of quasi-markets now found in many Western states develop. In the UK, for example, competitive independent providers are increasingly replacing monopolistic state agencies as service providers in the health sector and other social service spheres, but mediating agents such as professionals and purchasing authorities act on behalf of consumers in choosing a precise mix of services. Social policy change in China does not parallel that witnessed in the UK, but some aspects are common.

Perhaps the most direct form of market infiltration is adoption of cost-recovery as the central principle in determining service provision. In many social policy sectors state subsidy is now curtailed and consumers are expected to pay for what they need or want. Notable examples are private medicine, for-profit nursing homes, private schools and market housing. In each sector, access is effectively determined by ability to pay. It is often said that in a typical market transaction services are commodified because users bear the full cost of what they get without consideration of their needs, circumstances or citizenship status. Such transactions are becoming increasingly prevalent in Chinese social policy.

Behind these very obvious shifts towards the market lies an infiltration of public service management by business principles. As part of this process, state services are often contracted out, hived off or sold to private operators. Other reforms include decentralizing responsibility from the central state to local authorities and communities, increasing competition and efficiency, downsizing the public sector, and curtailing state functions.

A comparative context for Chinese social policy change

One context for contemporary social policy change in China – the status quo ante reform – has already been sketched. Another obvious context, already touched on in previous sections, is comparable change elsewhere. Social policy reform is, after all, a global process imbued with many common themes and concepts. Some concepts may be more appropriate descriptions of what is happening in some systems than in others. Some approaches may be articulated with more enthusiasm in some places than in others. Even within a single state, there may be important regional variations in the course taken by reform. Starting points differ, reform initiatives have distinct profiles, outcomes are multiple. Yet behind the many differences that undoubtedly characterize change in diverse local settings lie some elements of similarity. If we are to understand the nature of contemporary social policy reform, it is important to pay attention not only to distinct national and regional experiences, but also to shared themes and concepts. This book seeks to examine social policy reform in China in the context of broader reform debates and experience. It also attempts, where possible, to comment on the diversity of approaches and outcomes found across regions in the huge Chinese mainland.

A full comparative analysis of the social policy change now taking place in China is best left to the end of this exploration (see Chapter 7). However, at the outset some markers can be put down to set up that discussion. If we look at the development of social policy analysis in recent years we see, very crudely, that a Western focus on privatization and deconstruction of the welfare state in the 1980s has been replaced in the 1990s by an interest in ways in which the welfare state is being restructured. This shift chiefly reflects the reality of social policy change in the West, for (despite many predictions to the contrary) welfare states in Esping-Andersen's conservative, liberal and social democratic worlds have not been privatized to any significant extent (Esping-Andersen, 1990; Pierson, 1994). They have, however, been restructured in major ways as governments have sought to respond to international economic pressures by enhancing national competitiveness through efficiency drives or, sometimes, straightforward cost containment. At the start of the 1990s Cerny (1990) argued that what we were witnessing was a shift from welfare states to competition states. Others have since made very similar points. This shift certainly comprises the introduction of markets, quasi-markets and business practices to the operations of the state, but that is not the same thing as a shift from public to private sector. Indeed, in the three areas of state involvement on which Le Grand and Robinson (1984) built their mid-1980s analysis of privatization – provision, funding and regulation – the extent to which welfare states have been rolled back in the West remains quite limited.

Two predominant themes can be seen in the interest in structural adjustment that characterizes Western social policy analysis in the 1990s. One is a focus on what is often called the 'new public management' (Hood, 1991), and ways in which the institutions of the state are being reconfigured. The new public management can mean many and varied things, but at its heart is an attempt to change the culture of government by infusing it with the sorts of disciplines widely believed to be present in all parts of the private sector. In the West the profit motive has only rarely been built directly into public sector operations. Instead, a series of proxies for it has been developed in the wealth of performance measures that increasingly litter Western states. The intention is that such measures should generate the same sorts of incentive to efficient performance that are said to exist in business organizations. One consequence has been the creation of semi-autonomous units within the wider public sector that can be held to account for their performance. What that performance is expected to be is increasingly specified in contracts of one kind or another. The second theme is an attempt to get to grips with the major forces that lie behind the shift from welfare to competition states, and that are usually brought together under the general heading of globalization. Indeed, an emergent feature of contemporary social policy analysis is an international dimension relating to both main themes. Whilst the new public management literature initially focused chiefly on decentralization of responsibility and control, it has subsequently developed a parallel interest in supranational social policy structures, chiefly because of the growing involvement of the European Union (EU) in social policy spheres. Whilst the globalization literature started by looking at the impact of international finance and business, it is now extending its reach to encompass the role of international agencies in contributing to social policy change, notably in states outside Esping-Andersen's three worlds. Some of these agencies take the form of quasi-governmental institutions, notably the United Nations and World Bank. Others are international NGOs, such as Oxfam, the Save the Children Fund and so on (Deacon, 1997).

From a comparative perspective, the main task facing this volume is to determine the extent to which the global reform processes sketched here are reflected in Chinese experience. Put another way, the task is to identify the degree to which contemporary social policy change has Chinese 'characteristics' or, alternatively, conforms to some sort of international paradigm. This issue is picked up in each of the sectoral chapters that follows, and revisited in Chapter 7.

2
Labour Policy Reform

Grace O.M. Lee

Labour markets are central features of capitalist societies but are not supposed to be central to socialist societies. In the socialist society, the means of production are owned by the whole society; every person is a master of the means of production and everyone has the obligation and right to work (Feng, 1982, p.2). For many years after the Revolution of 1949, China sought to conform to the socialist paradigm. Since the late 1970s, however, reform initiatives have increasingly introduced labour markets into the Chinese economy. Because the Chinese Communist regime continues to deny an individual's private labour rights, treating them instead as a national resource, the terminology has often been contested. Until 1994 reform economists were careful to avoid direct use of the term 'labour market', preferring to use terms such as 'labour service market' (*laowu shichang*). The same squeamishness prompted the use of the term 'waiting for employment' instead of 'unemployment' before 1994. In addition, the Chinese reality has often been much more complex than any neat division would suggest (both pre- and post-reform). Nevertheless, there certainly has been change and that is what this chapter will investigate.

The chapter begins with a description of the pre-economic reform system in which state allocation of labour was the practice, and labour hoarding the norm. Following this, there is a description of the reform programme, stating the reasons for reform, and detailing the process of change (redefining the role of the state, diversifying the channels of labour allocation, and establishing a labour contract system). The chapter then moves to examine the impact of reform (broadening of work options, more flexible employment systems, labour mobility in terms of inter-plant mobility and inter-regional mobility, and unemployment). In analysing the pattern of change, several factors are found to explain why the real impact of labour reforms has so far fallen short of the reformers' intentions in the state sector (problems inherent in the policies themselves, blockages from within the state, and blockages in society). Towards the end of the chapter, it is concluded that a free labour market has re-emerged (since the rise of the Communist regime) in the non-state sector, and there is a discussion of the major impediments to the development of a free labour market in the state sector (the top political priority of stability, the absence of viable alternative sources of social security and livelihood needs outside the workplace, and the segmentation of labour according to expertise and household registrations).

The pre-reform system

A labour market has two important features: (a) employment is entered into on the basis of an agreement between employer and employee, and terminated on the initiative of both or either party (subject to any contractual conditions); (b) there is an exchange of labour power for a certain amount of remuneration, usually but not exclusively in the form of wages: labour power is sold as a commodity (White, 1987). Prior to the economic reforms in 1978, these features were not greatly in evidence. The allocation of labour resources was by far the furthest from the market mechanism. In accordance with the principle of 'unified employment and assignment', state labour bureaus at central and local levels exercised a virtual monopoly over the allocation of urban labour, including both manual workers and technical-professional staff in both state and 'big collective' sectors (White, 1987, p.115). The principle of 'unified allocation' or 'obey the arrangements of the organization' originated in 1950s, with regard to university and college graduates.

In the early 1950s, the Communist government had neither the time nor the capacity to control the labour market. Most firms were still managed by private owners. Government-issued labour regulations were mainly aimed at protecting the interests of employees, enhancing employees' collective bargaining power and limiting the employer's power by imposing new standards in the areas of dismissal, workers' compensation and labour safety (Zheng, 1987). In the mid-1950s, there was a remarkable shift in economic policy towards nationalization of industrial and commercial enterprises. By 1956, nearly all enterprises had been brought under the control of the state and collectives. The span of state control was broad and the machinery of administrative regulation was rigid. With few exceptions, state and collective enterprises hired employees through local labour bureaus. Job assignment was based on state planning, with little consideration for personal preferences. Employment through assignment was gradually extended to include all those entering the labour force, including demobilized army personnel. Labour mobility was tightly controlled, so inter-regional transfers – especially transfers from underdeveloped to comparatively developed areas – were very difficult if not impossible (Han and Morishima, 1992) owing to the household registration (*hukou*) and grain rationing systems. As a result of this highly rigid labour allocation system, it was not uncommon for husbands and wives to work in separate cities, hundreds or thousands of miles apart.

Young school leavers were assigned to a work-unit (*danwei*) which registered their citizenship status (*hukou*) (Cheng and Selden, 1994). This cultivated in young people a mentality of dependence, thinking that the state should give them jobs. Though in theory individuals were not committed to *danweis* against their will, refusal to join an officially assigned *danwei* could have serious repercussions, ranging from failure to find a permanent workplace to a politically tainted record. After job assignment, the individual found it hard to move from his or her original unit in the face of bureaucratic obstacles (inside and outside the enterprise) and other external controls, notably the *hukou* system and ration coupons. Mismatching of jobs to people often resulted in discontentment, and thereby poor productivity and low morale. As Shenkar and von Glinow stated, 'however disgruntled they may be, employees are reluctant to leave the work unit to which they have been assigned out of fear of remaining unaffiliated in a society in which major necessities are supplied only through organizational affiliation' (Shenkar and von Glinow, 1994, p.61). The enterprises run the society (*qiyie ban shehui*). The *danwei* constituted a mini welfare state, providing not only jobs and earnings but also a wide array of goods and services for employees and their families, including housing, medical care, educational provision, childcare and pensions. In the state-run factories, and to a moderately smaller degree in urban collective enterprises, a new form of relationship was institutionalized which Walder has characterized as a system of 'institutionalized clientelism; a neo-traditional pattern of authority based on citizen dependence on social institutions and their leaders' (Walder, 1986, p.8). Most workers and staff on the state payroll had lifetime tenure in their original units, with job promotions or wage increments based heavily on seniority.

Overstaffing had long been common in a labour surplus economy such as China. From the mid-1950s on, the Chinese party-state took upon itself the task of finding jobs for the vast majority of urban job-seekers. In consequence, particularly in periods of a 'high tide' in employment pressures (such as the late 1970s and early 1980s), state labour bureaus intensified problems of overstaffing in the state sector by forcing surplus urban labour power on to enterprises beyond their requirements. 'Five people do the job of three' was a popular saying during this period. This high degree of administrative intervention could be attributed to: (a) the ideological commitment to full employment, an implicit symbiosis on which the state would find it difficult to renege (White, 1987, p.116); (b) the tendency for enterprises to generate 'excess demand' (Kornai, 1980: ch. 1), seeking to enhance their ability to meet plan targets by building up hidden labour reserves and 'hoarding' labour; (c) the extreme difficulty in dismissing employees. The government told the workers that they were 'masters' (*zhuren*) in socialist China (Kaple, 1994, p.73). Being 'the master of the firm' meant that they could not be fired no matter how poorly they performed. The last two reasons were: (d) the 'stable' and 'safe' employment system which enhanced an inherent tendency towards nepotism; and (e) the practice of 'occupational inheritance' (*ding ti*). When a worker retired, he or she could recommend a close relative for his or her job. This practice probably led to overmanning on an extensive scale (Howe, 1992, p.ix). A classic case of such job inheritance was at the Anshan Iron and Steel Corporation (Byrd and Tidrick, 1987). Over 17 000 children replaced their parents over 1980–3, some of the latter retiring early. Some workers sought early retirement so that their children could take up their jobs. This led to a lowering of the technical and professional levels of the workers. Some workers often let the least competent of their sons and daughters take their jobs, which actually meant that this system of children replacing parents turned into a system of 'picking the worst' to employ (Feng, 1982, p.16).

Consequently, the unified employment and assignment system lowered the quality of the employees as a whole and was implemented at the expense of lowering labour productivity. Managers' power to dismiss workers and workers' motivations to move were both weak. In terms of job mobility, the consequences in urban China after 1960 were 'low levels of inter-firm transfers, high levels of regional and enterprise autarky, and risk averse strategies of advancement that discouraged firm switching' (Davis, 1992, p.1084). This was the oft decried 'iron rice-bowl' which reformers targeted as a major reason for poor productivity.

The reform programme

The Third Plenum of the Chinese Communist Party's Central Committee in 1978 introduced a comprehensive programme of sweeping changes to the previous system of economic planning and management in the urban-industrial sector. The main provisions for economic reform were twofold (Child, 1994, p.55). First, central planning and control over resource allocation, pricing and distribution were drawn back to permit the operation of market forces. Moreover, forms of non-state and foreign-funded enterprises were allowed to develop and these injected a powerful new competitive force into the economy. Second, new regulations and enactment had changed the formal provisions of industrial governance, as with the Director Responsibility and Contract Responsibility Systems, the 1988 Enterprise Law, and the regulations governing direct foreign investment. The reform agenda included changes in labour policy. At the macro level, movement towards the market in commodities and capital required similar movement towards the market in labour. At the micro level, it did not make sense to give enterprise managers greater power over production, marketing, procurement and investment without a similar extension of power to handle labour power.

In framing their labour policies, reform policy makers and analysts tried to increase labour flexibility by reducing the administrative stranglehold of the state over labour allocation and granting managers greater power to manage labour by weakening the 'iron rice-bowl'. It was hoped that the 'socialist commodity production' would, at the macro level, enhance allocative efficiency in two senses: economic and socio-political (White, 1987, p.118). From an economic viewpoint, a more flexible system of labour allocation would be more successful in matching labour supply and societal needs, both quantitatively and qualitatively (that is, allowing people to find not just any job, but the 'right' job). From a socio-political viewpoint, a more fluid system would be better able to match job openings and career structures with individual aspirations, thereby increasing job morale and labour productivity. Greater managerial powers over labour would allow enterprises to adapt more quickly to changing market conditions, would concentrate the workers' minds and would stimulate technical innovation and more cost-effective use of labour.

Process of change

The measures proposed by reformers to increase labour mobility in the urban-industrial context can conveniently be grouped under three headings: a reduction in the role of the state, diversification of channels of labour allocation, and the establishment of a new employment system in state enterprises based on contracts (White, 1987, pp.118–20).

Redefinition of the role of the state

One of the main thrusts of the reform programme was to redefine and reduce state regulation of the labour force. The principle of state planning was to remain dominant: that is, state labour bureaus would continue to regulate the overall proportions of the national labour force, but would reduce their direct interventions in the detailed process of labour allocation. As part of this process of 'destatification', state responsibility for the 'unified allocation' of certain strategic groups was to be gradually reduced. In the past, these groups – notably graduates of tertiary educational institutions and technical high schools, demobilized army officers and soldiers – had been guaranteed jobs, and their disposition was planned and executed on a nation-wide basis by direct administrative action by the central labour bureau in Beijing. Following the reform, more options were available. When the 'Reform Programme in the Job Assignment System of University/College Graduates' came into effect in March 1989, the university and college graduates could choose to join any enterprise which offered them a job. They could also visit enterprises to get information about particular jobs (Han and Morishima, 1992, p.237). Moreover, the role of local labour bureaus, which had been responsible for finding jobs for virtually all urban job-seekers in the past, was to change. Although bureaus were still responsible for overall labour planning, their role had shifted from administration to recommendation and intermediation. When applicants applied through the local labour bureaus for jobs, the labour bureaus would send the applications to relevant enterprises, together with the personnel files and evaluations (a student's political attitude and academic performance were evaluated before he or she left school). After short-listing the candidates, the enterprise would send the list to the local labour bureaus for approval. There was also a diversification of agencies involved in labour allocation.

Diversification of channels of labour allocation

The reformists texts talked of a 'three-in-one combination' of direct allocation by state labour bureaus, decentralized allocation by labour service companies, and a mixture of informally organized networks that encourage exchange in sectors such as self-employment. Self-employment, as a legitimate economic form, was written into the Constitution of the People's Republic of China in 1979 (Feng and Zhao, 1981, p.20). In 1980, an individual workers' association with a membership of 800 was founded in Nangang district of Harbin. This was the first individual workers' organization formed in China since 1949. It helped guarantee the interests of individual labourers and solved problems concerning the management and supply of raw materials for individual businesses (Feng and Zhao, 1981, p.20).

Labour service companies began to emerge in late 1978. For example, in Jilin in 1979, there was one labour service company on the municipal level, three on the district level and 40 on the neighbourhood level. In addition to offering literacy classes and vocational training courses for the jobless, they also operate[d] factories and service facilities, providing temporary jobs ... For instance, 43 per cent of the city's [Beijing] 42 000 temporary or permanent jobs assigned in 1979 were arranged with the help of these labour service companies ... [By 1981] two million people throughout the country [were] taking training courses or working within the framework of these companies – about 600 000 to 700 000 people [had] got permanent jobs, more than one million [had] temporary or seasonal work, and many others [were] taking vocational training courses.

(Feng and Zhao, 1981, p.21)

Although most of these companies remained under state supervision (many labour service companies were established under the supervision of street committees and state enterprises), they enjoyed a certain autonomy, both as labour exchanges and as centres of job creation (by setting up their own independent enterprises, usually in the form of shops, hotels or small factories). They were mainly involved in arranging jobs in the collective sector. In the state sector, while state labour bureaus still retained the power to set overall labour-force quotas, enterprise managers were to have greater power to choose what type of workers they wanted within the numeric quota.

The third element of the new 'three-in-one combination' was the attempt to increase the choice available to individual workers and professional staff, particularly the latter. A pioneer in this category was the Beijing Talent Exchange Centre. In 1989, it launched the Spring Labour Fair, bringing together 130 firms and 6000 potential workers. By 1992, attendance had grown tenfold. By 1993, even greater numbers, possibly over 100 000, attended a National Talent Fair (Warner, 1995, p.60). By 1998, these Talent Fairs had become very well established in cities such as Shenyang, Tianjin, Shanghai, Guangzhou, Xian, Wuhan and Chengdu (field interview, January 1998). Talent Fairs were also organized according to professions (for example, the Talent Fair for the

Weaving Industry held in Xian) and districts (for example, the Baoshan Talent Fair in Shanghai). Furthermore, recruitment could be made through advertisements in newspapers, on television, and through employment agencies.

Starting from 1994, the Regulations on Placement Service set standards for approval of applications in Shanghai, enforced by the Labour and Social Security Bureau (field interview, June 1999). One placement centre was to be set up for every 100 000 to 200 000 residents. The Shanghai Labour Bureau was contemplating standardizing the layout, logo and colour schemes of the placement centres, including staff uniforms. There were 452 registered employment agencies in Shanghai, of which 338 were established under the Labour Administration Division that included district and street organizations; 110 were operated by industries and social organizations such as trade unions, Association for the Handicapped, and the Women's Federation, and four were private operations. According to the deputy head of a District Labour Bureau in Shanghai, privately operated employment agencies were not encouraged. One reason was that they were profit making, while the employment agencies run by the state did not charge any fees, and those run by the various industries and organizations were run on a cost-recovery basis. The second reason was that private employment agencies were not able to provide comprehensive services to the job-seekers (field interview, June 1999).

The comprehensive services that were referred to by the government included counselling of job-seekers on market information, re-education for a change of mindset in abandoning the 'iron rice-bowl' mentality, and re-training in skills that were demanded by the market. A ranking of ten job types that were in demand would be advertised every week in the local newspaper, so that the general public could have access to labour market information and be more ready to engage in re-training. Training programmes would be offered for the first four job types that were in high demand: for example, cashiers working in stores and supermarkets that had mushroomed after the economic reforms. To establish rapport between the counsellor and his or her client, changing counsellor was not encouraged. Counters for individual counselling were set up based on the age, sex and health of the job-seekers, as well as the industries. All counsellors who worked in the placement system received training and were annually required to pass an examination. Overseas training in Germany was also arranged for outstanding staff. They needed to understand their clients and their family needs (for example, to arrange for baby-sitting or nursery care before

taking up employment), and to endorse applications for unemployment insurance. In a sense, the state closely monitored the workers
who were laid off by their enterprises. Workers had to go through the
various stages of job referrals, counselling and re-training. The payment of a subsistence allowance (*zhuidi shenghuo butei*) was not automatically granted, but would be subject to review at three-monthly
intervals. Yet the government was adamant about preserving social stability and instructed that all cases of hardship must be relieved. On top
of the distribution of subsistence allowances, the government subsidized the job-seeker's contributions to the state old-age pension and
medical insurance schemes. Counsellors who failed to spot such cases
would be penalized should their clients complain.

All the state established agencies were linked vertically (from city,
municipalities and districts to street organizations) and horizontally
among agencies at the same level. Starting from 1 July 1997, state-
operated employment agencies in Shanghai were inter-connected to
provide real-time information on the job market to job-seekers (field
interview, January 1998). In the past, enterprises that had vacancies
could only apply for labour through the government bureaus. At the
moment, enterprises need only register their vacancies with the placement centres; their vacancies will then be advertised through the inter-
linked net. The net also links nine employment agencies set up by the
industries themselves. Apart from displaying job vacancies, information
on re-training is also available on the net. In the case of Beijing, the city
was linked to its 18 districts in April 1995 at the cost of 8 million yuan.
Hence the labour markets for rural migrants, such as young women
seeking jobs as domestic servants (primarily from Anhui), could also be
reached (field interview, May 1998). To create more employment opportunities, the Shanghai Labour Bureau invested in minor environmental
improvement programmes at the district level. So far, over 20 000
vacancies have been created (field interview, May 1999).

The labour contract system

The third main area of reform, which was launched in early 1983, was
an effort to complement these system reforms by changes within the
enterprise. The most important of these was the attempt to 'break the
iron rice-bowl' of state workers by introducing the labour contract system. This reform aimed to increase the discretionary powers of managers over their workforce, in particular strengthening their ability to
dismiss workers. In the past, virtually all state workers had enjoyed job
security; henceforth, they would be employed on contracts of varying

lengths, signed between themselves and their enterprise and enforceable through new labour legislation. The new system of employee contracting began as experiments in Shanghai and the Special Economic Zones (SEZs) in 1980. By 1983, the Ministry of Labour issued temporary regulations and circulars to set guidelines for contract systems and called for their universal extension to all new workers in state-owned and collectively-owned enterprises. By October 1986, State Council temporary regulations further formalized these changes into the 'Contractual Responsibility System' (Westwood and Leung, 1996, pp.377–8). The core principles of this reform were to (a) introduce a labour contract system by which workers were employed on a contractual basis and no longer as 'permanent' employees with virtual lifetime guarantees; (b) establish a more open and rational recruitment system and dissolve the system of giving recruitment priority to the children of existing work unit members; (c) give enterprises the right to terminate the employment of inadequately performing workers; (d) establish systems of social security and old-age pension schemes that were at least partly contributory; (e) allow non-profitable enterprises to be declared bankrupt (Korzec, 1988, pp.117–49). At the end of the contract, if the worker's performance had been unsatisfactory or if the labour needs of the enterprise had altered in response to market fluctuations or technological change, the contract need not be renewed. In addition to increasing the flexibility of managerial controls over labour, it was hoped that this system would improve labour productivity by increasing the motivation to work under the stimulus of job insecurity. The enterprises, labour service companies and local governments would each play a role in providing welfare benefits (which had formerly been the sole responsibility of the enterprise) and in retraining and redeploying redundant workers.

Impact of reform

Broadening work options

One important impact of reform is a general broadening of work options. SOEs, although still a major source of employment, are no longer the only choice available. There are collective and private enterprises and increasing numbers are pursuing the entrepreneurial track, with government encouragement (the existence of private enterprises was legitimized with the amendment to the Constitution in 1988). Furthermore, employment opportunities exist in Sino-foreign joint

Table 2.1   Number of employees working in units of various ownership, 1996

Type of ownership	Number of employees (in ten thousands)
Urban Area	
State-owned units	11 244
Urban collective-owned units	3 016
Joint-owned economic units	49
Shareholding economic units	363
Foreign-funded economic units	275
Economic units funded by entrepreneurs from Hong Kong, Macau and Taiwan	265
Units of other types of Ownership	9
Private enterprises	620
Individuals	1 709
Rural Area	
Township/village enterprises	13 508
Private enterprises	551
Individuals	3 308

Source: *Zhongguo Tongji Nianjian* (*China Statistical Yearbook*), 1997, pp.96–7.

ventures or wholly-owned foreign companies. Table 2.1 shows that the number of employees working in the non-state sector actually outnumbered that of the state sector in 1996.

A closer look at the statistics in Table 2.1 reveals that the number of employees working in TVEs was comparable to the total number of employees working in the state sector (including state-owned units and urban collective-owned units). Hence it should be useful and interesting to examine the composition of TVEs, as shown in Table 2.2.

More flexible employment system

Since the economic reforms, the employment system has become relatively more flexible, though only by degrees and by sector. Outside the state sector, the job status of workers and the flow of labour are much closer to the notion of the labour market. Ip's study (1998) suggested that 'an emerging labor market is functioning in the Shenzhen SEZ, in the wake of a state engineered transformation from a state omnipotent economy to a "market economy with socialistic characteristics"'

Table 2.2 Types and employment of township and village enterprises, 1996

	Number of enterprises	Number of employees
Agriculture	289 444	3 359 955
Industry	7 564 336	78 601 383
Construction	1 045 824	19 488 380
Transport	5 464 886	10 623 245
Commerce	5 948 610	13 845 798
Restaurants	1 668 475	5 397 361
Tourism	835 561	2 003 124
Others	516 149	1 763 605
Total	23 333 285	135 082 851

Source: *Zhongguo Xiangzhen Qiye Nianjian* (*Chinese Township and Village Enterprises Statistical Yearbook*), 1997, pp.124–5.

(1998, p.301). On the labour market supply side, workers have considerable freedom over their choice of employment. In contrast to the inflexible monolithic state allocation system that dominated the pre-reform era, workers enjoy multiple avenues in their search for jobs: self-initiated calls, street posters, word of mouth and personal recommendations from friends and relatives and so on. In 1990, about 70 per cent of total employment was secured through market mechanisms (Chang, 1994, p.87). On the demand side, employers adopt market and profit-driven policies. With costs and the imperatives of the labour market in mind, employers utilize various modes of recruitment and reward systems to secure workers in short supply (such as technical workers) as opposed to workers in plentiful supply (such as semi-skilled and unskilled workers). To compete for skilled workers that are in short supply, enterprises offer favourable terms including high wages, housing and other fringe benefits. In some instances, employers offer to help in the transfer of household registrations as incentives to recruit and retain high calibre workers. Table 2.3 clearly indicates the growing tendency for new urban employees to prefer the non-state sector.

While the number of new entrants to the state sector declined by a third, the number joining the non-state sector more than doubled over the period from 1991 to 1996. One attraction of the non-state sector could be higher wages. The average money wage per annum among the state-owned units, urban collective owned units and units of other types of ownership were 6280 yuan, 4302 yuan and 8261 yuan

Table 2.3   New urban employees (grouped by employment), 1991–96 (in ten thousands)

Year	State sector		Non-state sector	
	State-owned units	Urban collective-owned units	Other ownership units	Urban individual labourers
1991	363.0	272.0	70.0	60.0
1992	366.9	218.2	77.5	73.4
1993	310.0	202.0	98.0	95.0
1994	294.0	181.0	115.0	135.0
1995	260.0	170.0	155.0	135.0
1996	243.0	155.0	167.0	140.0

Source: *Zhongguo Laodong Tongji Nianjian* (*Chinese Labour Statistical Yearbook*), 1997, p.8.

respectively in 1996 (*Zhongguo Tongji Nianjian*, 1997, p.123). Another major attraction of a joint venture was the offer of greater opportunities, especially in terms of personal and professional learning about Western business and management styles and techniques (Westwood and Leung, 1996, pp.395–6), a recognition of the skills deficiencies in the labour market and as a means of securing a competitive advantage.

Labour mobility

Another indicator of a free labour market is mobility of labour. Leaving jobs voluntarily in favour of better paid ones became a trend among workers. Wage inducements were made possible. Wages and working conditions seemed to direct the movement of labour from low to high waged jobs. Labour exchanges were set up and private firms were free to recruit freely. In the early 1990s, job transfers became easier. In 1992, nearly one million technical and managerial personnel registered at personnel exchange centres in order to seek relocation. Many qualified young graduates would like to work in joint ventures. According to the statistics of the Beijing Talent Exchange Centre, 70 per cent of the 4000 technical professionals who landed successful job transfers moved from state-owned enterprises to non state-owned enterprises (Westwood and Leung, 1996, p.88). In Shanghai, which has nearly 1000 substantially sized foreign-funded enterprises, half their employees were hired by such personnel agencies (*Beijing Review*, 1 February 1993, p.13). It was estimated that as many as one in three professionals would like to move their place of employment, but that might not be easy for skilled professionals who were of value to their employment units, which might be reluctant to release them. The problem was also acute in the civil service system. Some civil service applicants, though offered an appointment, were refused permission to leave their original units and were unable to assume the new posts (Dai, 1994, p.200). Very often, the mere request from the enterprise for the return of living quarters was bad enough to discourage inter-firm mobility. Therefore, the actual transfer rate was probably around 3–4 per cent. Although arbitration boards were set up in major cities to deal with appeals against enterprises refusing individual transfers, few employee plaintiffs won their case (field interview, May 1998).

In addition to inter-plant mobility, there was also evidence of rapidly increasing inter-regional labour mobility, both within and between provinces. Increasing numbers of peasants were allowed into the larger cities on temporary contractual employment. By the end of 1996, around 98 per cent of state-owned enterprises and collective enterprises (2240 enterprises) in Shanghai had entered into contracts with their employees (field interview, January 1998). Labour contracts were also common in economic organizations such as township industries, joint ventures and privately- and/or foreign-owned firms. In the mid-1980s, a 'floating' population – estimated at over 30 million people – entered the large coastal cities (Christiansen, 1992, p.74). The labour force in these instances was more likely to be young, and/or female, as well as of recent rural origin (Wong and Lee, 1996, p.213). They were absorbed by the urban economy in building, trade and petty services such as nannies. The main strategy of the government was to absorb rural surplus labour into TVEs, usually in the vicinity of the peasants' home villages. According to the decree 'The State Council Circular on the Problem of Peasants' Settlement in Market Towns' issued in 1984, peasants were permitted to transfer their *hukou* to market towns so long as they managed to find employment, maintain a stable residence and take care of their own food rations (Wong and Huen, 1998).

The massive flow of labour power was under far less regulation than in the urban sector and much more closely resembled a real labour market. For example, in Qixia Zhen near Nanjing, there were about 300 non-locals employed by family enterprises, constituting about 7 per cent of the local rural labour force (Christiansen, 1992, p.78). Although this number was not big, it did indicate that the private and individual enterprises in the countryside had helped create a situation in which the rural labour market transcended village and township boundaries, making it easier for individual labourers to move to non-local workplaces. The private and individual enterprises in the urban areas had similar pattern of 'open' labour recruitment across formal boundaries (jurisdiction and household registration system). This is best illustrated with a concrete example:

> A small private restaurant in the centre of Nanjing employs a retired cook from a state-owned restaurant, four or five very young peasant women who are waitresses, and some state employees who supplement their wages with odd jobs in the private sector. The cook earns about 500 yuan a month plus fringe benefits, which exceeds his retirement pension by 500 per cent; the young women and the state employees earn a handsome 150 to 200 yuan per month plus other, unspecified benefits ... The impact of such enterprises on the labour market is great, since they open a route for peasants into urban areas.
>
> (Christiansen, 1992, p.81)

This is a significant consequence of the reforms, but this new and more 'open' market is not genuinely open. It is still fragmented, because it is limited to the private and individual enterprise sector, and labour migration is restricted by the household registration system. The result is that such labour migration is temporary. The country girls in the restaurant cited in the above example do not become legal urban residents, nor do they register as temporary residents. They belong to the so-called floating population; its numbers are extremely difficult to estimate.

Unemployment

Another impact of the labour policy reform is unemployment (*shiye*). The concept of unemployment was acknowledged by the Chinese authorities as a common characteristic of a commodity economy only in 1994. Before that, the situation was described as 'waiting for employment' (*daiye*). In Mao's era, the Communists distinguished between socialist *daiye* and capitalist *shiye*. The State Statistical Bureau (SSB) considered residents in cities and towns who had reached their economically productive age, who were able-bodied and motivated to work, but who could not find a job and were registered at the local labour authorities or in street organizations as 'people waiting for employment'. The term 'unemployment rate' was used for the first time in February 1994 after the announcement of the 'Report on

National Social and Economic Development for 1993' (*Inside Mainland China*, August 1995). However, the definition of unemployment is distinctive in China. According to the SSB, open unemployment refers to the urban registered unemployed who (a) possess a non-agricultural residence, (b) are within a certain age range (16–50 for male and 16–45 for female), (c) are able and willing to work, and (d) have registered with the local labour bureau for employment (*China Labour Statistical Yearbook*, 1997, p.588). The openly unemployed are eligible for unemployment benefits.

According to the statistics of the Ministry of Labour, the unemployment rate was 2.8 per cent in 1994 and 2.9 per cent in late 1995. In 1996, the State Statistical Bureau recorded an unemployment rate of 3 per cent (5.5 million registered unemployed). At the end of 1997, the unemployment rate rose to 3.1 per cent (5.8 million registered unemployed). Table 2.4 shows the registered urban unemployed and unemployment rate from 1978 to 1997.

Table 2.4 Registered urban unemployed and unemployment rate, 1978–97

Year	Number of unemployed urban workers (millions)	Unemployment rate (%)
1978	5.30	5.3
1979	5.67	5.4
1980	5.42	4.9
1981	4.40	3.8
1982	3.79	3.2
1983	2.71	2.3
1984	2.36	1.9
1985	2.39	1.8
1986	2.64	2.0
1987	2.77	2.0
1988	2.96	2.0
1989	3.78	2.6
1990	3.83	2.5
1991	3.52	2.3
1992	3.64	2.3
1993	4.20	2.6
1994	4.76	2.8
1995	5.20	2.9
1996	5.53	3.0
1997	5.77	3.1

Source: *Zhongguo Tongji Nianjian* (*China Statistical Yearbook*), various years; *Laodong Neican*, July 1998, p.15.

Another type of unemployment is referred to as 'hidden unemployment', concerning workers who are laid off (*xiagang*). The State Statistical Bureau defines laid-off workers to be 'workers who have left their posts and are not engaged in other types of work in the same unit, but [who] still maintain a labour relationship with the unit [where] they have worked' (*CLSY*, 1997, p.588). Workers who have been laid off are only given living subsidies (*shenghuofei*) instead of unemployment benefits, and are not included in the registered unemployment rate. The State Statistical Bureau has kept statistics on workers laid off since 1995. The number of laid-off workers rose from 5.6 million in 1995 to 8.1 million in 1996. It further increased to about 10 million by the end of June 1997 (*CLSY*, 1996, p.406; 1997, p.405; 1998, p.314). In 1998, the Ministry of Labour and Social Security predicted that the state enterprises would lay off 8–10 million workers over the next three years (*China Daily – Business Weekly*, 26 April 1998, p.8).

Workers in state enterprises, particularly those approaching the age of retirement and women, have been the worst hit by restructuring. In the pre-reform era, state workers were the labour aristocrats of Chinese socialism (Walder, 1986). However, as a result of more than a decade of urban market reforms, they have been unceremoniously dethroned. The introduction of wage reforms, the labour contract system and the establishment of a social security system have meant that state workers no longer enjoy a lifelong entitlement to employment but now work under a market-oriented contract. According to the State Statistical Bureau, women accounted for 59.2 per cent of the laid-off workers and 52.3 per cent of the registered unemployed in 1996 (*CLSY*, 1997, p.94). These people also found it much more difficult to become reintegrated into society. In the city of Shenyang alone, 49 316 women employees had officially been laid off (Kernen, 1997, p.18). Women made up 60 per cent of the unemployed in Liaoning. Research by a sociologist from the Liaoning Academy of Social Sciences showed that these were primarily women over 35, with a low educational level. Early retirement has become the norm since 1994. The retirement age has been lowered to 42 for women and 52 for men. Furthermore, for several years, women have been entitled to extended leave for up to seven years after the birth of their child. Most women, however, have not chosen to stop working, but have instead been pushed off the labour market. Although they received a small monthly allowance of 80–120 yuan, they lost much of their pay and most social benefits. Despite some progress in social insurance aimed at establishing sources of welfare outside the workplace, these alternatives were inadequate (Wong and Lee, 1996).

In a situation of heightened social tensions, workers frequently demonstrated in front of their municipal government offices. According to police statistics in Beijing, 80 per cent of the 12 000 demonstrations, petitions and traffic hold-ups inventoried in 1995 were caused by urban poverty. The crisis also showed up in other ways: suicide, divorce, petty crime and prostitution were on the increase. In an attempt to allay popular discontent, the municipal governments had been making a show of sympathy for the worst-off. The mayor and his subordinates visited the poor each year before the New Year, bearing coal, fruit, cakes and money. Throughout the year, 'give a bit of warmth' (*song wennuan*) campaigns were organized. As a result, despite the reformers' wish to see the boat go faster, they are also afraid of rocking it.

Analysis of the pattern of change

Several factors explain why the real impact of labour reforms has so far fallen short of reformers' intentions in the state sector: (a) problems inherent in the policies themselves; (b) blockages from within the state; and (c) blockages in society.

Problems inherent in the policies themselves

Some of the problems of labour reforms lie in the nature of the policies themselves. In the case of the attempt to introduce a labour contract system, for example, the official policy was very ambiguous, allowing lower administrative agencies and enterprises a great deal of room for manoeuvre in interpreting the policies as they saw fit (White, 1987, p.122). There are now signs that the labour system is evolving much more rapidly in the 1990s than in the middle and late 1980s. The main vehicle of such change was the 'Temporary Regulations on the Use of Labour Contracts in State-run Enterprises' enacted in October 1986. Henceforth, new recruits would not hold jobs for life, but would be given contracts for defined periods of employment. Other 'Temporary Regulations' originating at the same time covered employment in state enterprises, the sacking of personnel violating labour discipline, and insurance for employees 'waiting for employment' in state firms. The new regulations enabled state enterprises to decide 'the time, conditions, methods and numbers when hiring new employees' and to adopt 'the contracted management or all-personnel labour contract system' (*Beijing Review*, 16 November 1992, p.14). Firms would hire through examinations. Wages would be fixed by enterprises according both to performance levels and regulations, with freedom to arrive at the total sum for bonuses. Yet, in reality, there are problems inherent in the policies themselves.

In theory, contracts mean voluntary bilateral choices: managers gain new licence to dismiss workers while workers enjoy new freedom to switch jobs. However, in practice so far, the opportunity to move to better-paying firms is limited to younger, male, skilled and educated state workers, many of whom provided the 'technical backbone' for their original enterprise and left their state enterprises in the early 1990s when the labour contract reform was implemented. Managers and workers observe that today only 'the old, the sick, and women' stay until they are laid off or made redundant (Lee, 1999, p.56). In order to minimize potential social instability following massive and arbitrary redundancy, Guangzhou officials have issued regulations to circumscribe managers' autonomy to dismiss labour:

> For instance, they are prohibited from firing a worker whose spouse is already an off-duty or unemployed worker in another SOE. Veteran workers with more than ten years of continuous job tenure and who are within five years of retirement age are likewise protected from 'economic dismissal'. Enterprises, which dismiss employees, must have proven financial difficulties and must give priority to rehiring their own redundant workers when the business environment improves.
>
> (Lee, 1999, p.56)

The scope of enterprises that are subject to the above prohibitions and restrictions has actually extended from state enterprises to foreign enterprises. In Nanking, the following categories of workers cannot be retrenched by foreign enterprises (*Ming Pao*, 1999): (a) family of those serving in the armed forces; (b) workers who are partially disabled due to occupational injuries or disease; (c) workers who are on sick leave; (d) female workers on maternity leave; (e) workers who are due to retire in ten years' time or less; (f) if both husband and wife are serving in the same enterprise, only one party can be dismissed; (g) workers protected by the collective agreement from retrenchment; (h) workers protected by the various laws and regulations from dismissal. The regulation also stipulates that foreign enterprises that make workers redundant must recruit, with priority, from the pool of workers dismissed, within six months of the date of redundancy. Such restrictions on managerial discretion and autonomy are not consistent with the series of reforms in fostering a free labour market and greater entrepreneurial responsibility.

Furthermore, in spite of the greater powers given to state enterprises in recruiting labour, they must still answer to local labour bureaus on personnel questions, often against their own best interests. Francis (1996) suggested that the pattern of collective responsibility characteristic of the traditional work unit system has, to an extent, persisted within certain sectors of the market economy.

> Managers [of high-tech enterprises in the non-state sector] described being held informally responsible by local government authorities for the behavior of their employees. They reported that if one of their employees were arrested for a legal violation or public disturbance, local public security officials would expect them to mediate in resolving the matter ... In addition to fining the company, the public security bureau officials lectured the company representative about the company's responsibility for proper supervision and discipline of its employees.
>
> (Francis, 1996, p.855)

Blockages from within the state

To reduce the historical burden of state-owned enterprises, reformers promoted contract-based employment relations, enhanced the mobility of labour and established a societal-level safety net. Reforms concerning old age pensions, medical care, unemployment and housing have been implemented. The new safety net is to be built by pooling contributions from the state, the enterprise and the individual employee into unified social insurance funds. Enterprises of all ownership types are covered and the funds will be administered and allocated by local labour insurance companies. The intention is that older state enterprises with the most retirees or a high percentage of female workers could then take advantage of contributions from non-state sectors that have a younger, less welfare-dependent workforce. Because workers hold personal passbooks recording the amount of their individual contributions, they can supposedly change jobs and continue their insurance fund accumulation with their new employers. Nevertheless, there are many gaps in the new safety net:

> Uneven implementation of social insurance reform is most apparent in the non-state sector ... Moreover, with so many industrial enterprises suffering from chronic debt problems and making losses, the insurance funds are operating in deficit ... One prominent cause of this shortfall in the fund is the alleged 'short-term behaviour' of

managers in SOEs who refuse to see the enterprise wage bill used to meet future or other firms' pay-outs. The local press has accused them of under-reporting both the total number of workers and the total wage bill, or of opening multiple bank accounts to evade the burden of insurance contributions. Another prominent problem is official abuse of pension funds in the form of diversion and embezzlement. In 1997, nine cadres in Shenzhen's social insurance department, for instance, were found guilty of stealing 20 million yuan from the funds. The problem is so widespread that in 1998 the Labour and Social Security Ministry created a Social Insurance Funds Supervision Department to scrutinize local accounts and investigate their collection and use. In short, even though state insurance legislation is supposed to relieve workers from dependence on any particular enterprise by guaranteeing a certain minimum level of livelihood independent of participation in production, workers at the present moment confront the stark reality of finding themselves trapped in a 'transition gap' between two systems (enterprise insurance and state insurance) – a transition which some suggest will take another ten to 15 years to complete.

(Lee, 1999, p.48)

Blockages in society

Managerial opinion was also divided as to the merits of labour contracts (White, 1987, pp.381–2). Where skills were at a premium, say in capital-intensive enterprises, managers were loath to let workers go and many preferred the old system. They were even keener to hold on to professional staff. In less skill-intensive firms such as textile mills, managers tended to prefer contracts. Older managers were anxious to keep the labour system they had grown used to; younger managers were keen to change it. Reaction on the workers' side was mixed. Those in a seller's market, such as trained graduates, were keener to take their chances with the new system. To many of the state workforce, innovations such as the labour contract system were steps in the direction of 'capitalist wage labour'. According to a survey carried out by the All-China Federation of Trade Unions, claiming a sample of 210 000 workers from over 400 enterprises, only around one in eight (12.2 per cent) was able to display a high level of 'enthusiasm' in their work because of the labour contract system (Warner, 1995, pp.66–7). Seven out of eight (87.8 per cent) responded that they could only have mediocre or inadequate levels of motivation. Over one in three (36.3 per cent) thought they had no sense of being 'masters' in their enterprises;

half (51.5 per cent) thought workers' status was unduly low; and the rest believed they had virtually become 'hired hands'. Low enthusiasm among workers was principally reflected in the following: (a) low attendance rates; (b) low utilization rate of working hours, which was not above 50 per cent; (c) low labour enthusiasm and unwillingness to learn professional skills; (d) low labour productivity; and (e) low political enthusiasm where workers were not eager to join the youth league or the party, but only to pursue material interests. Hence, some reform economists were sceptical of the value of the labour contract system and saw it as a threat to the 'socialist nature' of state enterprises.

Worse still, various forms of everyday non-compliance inside state factories have the aggregate consequence of constraining the capacity of the state to implement its policies (Lee, 1998, p.9). To take the example of wage reforms:

> Promoting the principle of 'pay according to work,' factory directors adopt piece rate wage systems, introduce bonuses and efficiency rewards, and impose fines for faulty production, thereby creating wage differentials among workers. Although these are designed to push workers to work hard and raise productivity, they have elicited varying responses from workers. When the amount of workers' pay-cheques falls beyond what they consider a fair wage level, collective goldbricking, withdrawal of effort, spontaneous work stoppages and quasi sit-ins appear.
>
> (Lee, 1998, p.9)

This is because the official commitment to full employment since the revolution has created a strong political relationship, an implicit social contract, between the Chinese state and its urban constituents. A kind of institutionalized patron–client relationship has been established wherein the state assumed the role of provider and the urban population has come to depend on the state and to expect its largesse. If this relationship is threatened, if the state is seen to renege on its commitment to full employment, its legitimacy suffers and there is a danger of mass discontent and protest. Indeed, more than 10000 people chanted 'We want food, we want jobs' (*'yao chifan, yao gongzuo'*) in two protests in Sichuan and Heilongjiang, which resulted in more than 10 deaths and a few hundred people imprisoned (field interview, May 1998). As a matter of fact,

> All over China, millions of workers born into the 'iron rice bowl' system, of cradle-to-grave employment and state social services are

discovering that life no longer offers the certainties it once did. Socialism 'with Chinese characteristics' means that managers of state-owned enterprises have now been told by central government that their factories must stop losing money. They have looked at their overmanned production lines, and for the first time have been allowed to conclude that fewer people, working properly, could get the job done... China's underemployed workforce, who had grown lazy on the knowledge that – under communism – a job was for life, is now facing a new scourge: unemployment. And the authorities are facing up to the social unrest this may cause.

(Poole, 1993, p.14)

Conclusion

The notion of labour has been conceived very differently in capitalist and socialist economies. Labour was considered a national resource instead of an individual's private right in a socialist economy. Hence in the pre-reform era, labour was allocated to the different *danweis* and there was the absence of a labour market. Neither the *danwei* nor the individual, in principle, had the right to choose (that is, they could not refrain from accepting the state arrangement). Full employment was achieved through administrative measures of labour allocation, at the cost of inefficiencies. When, in the late 1970s, China opened its doors to the world economy, labour flexibility became necessary and the administrative control of the state over labour had to be reduced. The role of the state has been redefined from direct allocation to acting as an intermediary between the employer and the employee. The channels of labour allocation have been diversified to include self-employment and employment agencies. Labour reforms over the years do confirm the ideological acceptance of labour as a commodity, and marketization of labour is made possible. The individual, instead of the state, owns his or her labour power, and can enter into employment contracts. The scope of job choice and labour mobility has been expanded. Both employers and employees rely on the market mechanisms in the employment process and inter-firm mobility is possible.

It is evident that a relatively free labour market has re-emerged in the non-state sector (since the rise to power of the Communist regime). However, in the case of state agencies, the degree of administrative control over labour planning and allocation by means of directive methods remains high. State labour bureaus at various levels still dominate the process of labour allocation, although a good deal of their previous responsibility for the details has been devolved to other institutions, notably employment agencies and enterprises. There are three major impediments to the development of a free labour market in the state sector: (a) the top political priority of stability; (b) the absence of viable alternative sources of social security and livelihood needs outside the workplace; (c) the segmentation of labour according to expertise and household registration (*hukou*).

The first obstacle is the top political priority of stability. Despite empowering the directors of state enterprises to manage their own human resources (such as the setting-up of new wage systems and contract-based employment), these policies have been contradicted by the various restrictions placed on laying off workers. The same political concern for stability plus a need for loyalty from the armed forces applies to the demobilization of the army. Even though options are open for the demobilized army officers and soldiers to find their own jobs, and the Ministry of Personnel is to assume the role of an intermediary, for instance, in organizing the annual Job Bazaar for them to have direct contact with the representatives of the recruiting enterprises (normally state-owned enterprises), those military personnel who have not been offered a job will still rely on state allocation, and the state enterprises are obliged to fulfil their 'social responsibility' (field interview, June 1999).

The second obstacle is an institutional legacy of the traditional *danwei* system. The work unit's central role in providing for the material needs of employees in the earlier system critically shaped employees' dependence on their firms. Their work units, which impose financial obligations on them, often hold on to their skilled and talented employees, making it extremely costly for them to leave their jobs. Employees in state-owned enterprises will simply lose their housing if they leave their work unit. So even though the state employees are willing to seek alternative employment and are offered jobs, their job mobility is heavily dependent on the discretion of their original work units. On the other hand, the less marketable employees, though redundant, cannot be insensitively dismissed because of the inadequate provisions of social security. This first obstacle can virtually be removed with the trend of monetarization of benefits in contrast to the direct provision of services characteristic of traditional *danwei*. With the abolition of housing provision since 1 July 1998 (field interview, May 1998) and the setting-up of state insurance schemes, there are signs of remedy for this problem (though it may take a considerable number of years), but the second obstacle seems likely to remain in the foreseeable future.

The third obstacle to a free flow of labour is the segmentation of human resources into distinct categories of 'labour' (the unskilled and semi-skilled workers), 'talents' (the technical and professional staff), and 'cadres' (administrative personnel). The unskilled and semi-skilled workers are offered help by placement centres established under the Ministry of Labour; the 'talents' are supported by the Ministry of Personnel; and the 'cadres' (such as directors of state-owned enterprises) are to be recruited by the Central Organization Department. Such artificial categorization of human resources creates barriers to inter-job transfers and inconsistencies in employment policies. It would be more efficient if all employment services fell under the jurisdiction of one single ministry to enhance free flow of labour. However, the political intricacies that surround the issue make it insurmountable in the foreseeable future.

Another man-made cartel in opposition to free labour mobility is the household registration (*hukou*) system. Nevertheless, 'talents' are not subject to *hukou* restrictions. They can change their household registration if they manage to find a job in another place (field interview, June 1999). On the other hand, 'labourers' cannot change their *hukou* even if they are employed, and are treated as migrant workers. Even though a new household registration status (called the 'blue chop' or 'blue chop household registration') has been introduced in a number of cities since the late 1980s to grant a status between temporary residency and permanent household registration, the scheme is extremely selective and the new registration does not grant the privileges of urban living: namely, jobs and housing (Wong and Huen, 1998). In order to tackle the problem of unemployment, quotas have been set by most cities to limit the employment of workers who do not possess the 'proper' household registrations. In the case of Beijing, a 'quota for the employment of non-Beijing household registrants' (*liaojing zhibiao*) has been set to limit the employment of the 'outsiders' by enterprises. These non-Beijing household registrants are only allowed to fill around 230 job types that are detested by the local inhabitants (field interview, May 1998). Hence, labour is segmented not by individual competitiveness in terms of skills and knowledge, but by the *hukou* system. The development of a free labour market has been curtailed by such man-made rigidities. Discrimination and unequal treatment based on *hukou* is certainly an area to look into as regards future labour reforms in China.

In fact, the development of a labour market is essential in changing the value system of the people to cope with a modern society. Inkeles, Broaded and Cao argue that 'the lack of a free labour market in which individuals regard educational achievements as having the *potential* to make a real difference in their adult occupational status seems to be the most important factor in explaining Chinese education's failure to inculcate modern attitudes and values' (1997, p.56). In the post-Mao reform era, a highly stratified education system has been recreated (see Chapter 5 below). Those fortunate enough to enter the small number of 'keypoint' schools (*zhongdian xuexiao*) might see their education pay off in access to universities and in a better job placement. But for the vast majority of the urban youth in non-key academic schools or vocational schools, how long they stay in school and how well they perform as students has very little effect on their adult occupational placement. Job placement is primarily in the hands of municipal, district or neighbourhood labour bureaus. Many people who have finished high school are arbitrarily assigned to jobs as ordinary workers and sometimes even to menial positions as sweepers and cleaners. As a consequence, the attitude that studying is useless (*dushu wuyong*), which had been prevalent during the Cultural Revolution decade, was very widespread among non-elite urban school students in the 1980s. Many village parents also saw little advantage in sending their children to school if the only opportunities available to them were in agriculture and rural factories. Hence, greater freedom of movement means that educated rural children have more opportunities to enter the cities than was the case under the collective agriculture system.

A free labour market in which educational achievements or credentials more clearly affect people's occupational opportunities thus may be a macro structural prerequisite before formal schooling can promote the adoption of modern attitudes and values. Furthermore, employees working in the more marketized elements of the economy hold more modern attitudes. The contrast is especially large between industrial workers in urban state-run enterprises and industrial workers in township and village factories (Inkeles, Broaded and Cao, 1997, p.49). State enterprise fosters in its workers a basic conservatism and lack of dynamism. Rather than develop a sense of individual responsibility, the state enterprise seems to stimulate shifting responsibility to others. Workers in state enterprises are more likely to rely on government planning. On the other hand, the well being of workers in the more marketized economy depends directly and immediately on how hard they work, how well they plan their activities and how much individual initiative and responsibility they assume. Hence, the development of free labour market facilitates the progression of individual modernity and should indeed be supported.

3
Welfare Policy Reform
Linda Wong

When China opted for economic reform in 1978, its welfare system was part and parcel of the old socialist economy. Public ownership of the means of production in industry and agriculture provided the basis for life support. The rural hinterland was organized into people's communes which provided work for the peasants as well as social and welfare programmes in the local community. Welfare for urban residents was tied to work. The proverbial work unit, or *danwei,* gave support to its employees from 'head to toe' and 'from cradle to grave'. Only the destitute who did not belong to families or enterprises required state and neighbourhood relief. Such unfortunate persons were very few in number. Organized dependence on work and state agencies was celebrated as the victory of socialism.

This valuation changed with the reassessment of the state economy after the demise of radical Maoism. New reform leaders were appalled by the shambles produced by three decades of socialist planning. Measured against the standards of other countries, the Chinese economy stood out as backward and suffering from dire shortages. The blame was pinned on the lack of incentives, and the rigidity and inefficiency of a planned economy that responded more to planners' whims than to needs of the people. As systems of production and welfare were intertwined, post-Mao reformers included the welfare system in their critique of socialist economy. General weaknesses entailed 'encouraging dependence, flaccidity and free-riding' (known as 'eating from the same pot'). Consequently a new system was called for which would be compatible with the new market economy (White, 1998, p.178).

Specifically, socialist welfare was imbued with a number of deficiencies. In rural areas, the abolition of communes removed the collective basis for communal welfare. After peasants were given freedom to farm, work and conduct business as they pleased, welfare support had to be re-established within the locality. In comparison, the urban welfare apparatus was deemed to be in greater need of reform. First, the protection afforded by life-time employment and work-based benefits tied workers to their employers. As a result, labour could not move freely between jobs and occupations. Second, rewarding employees equally with no regard for effort and performance resulted in passivity and low productivity. Third, enterprise welfare had proved too costly. Many state firms were sagging under the bills for pensions, healthcare, housing and collective amenities which ruined their chances of competing with private and village enterprises that offered none of these perks. The state-owned sector would be doomed if the welfare burden could not be reduced or removed. All these factors made the transfer of employee welfare functions to other agencies necessary. Moreover, economic restructuring of socialist enterprises, including efficiency drives and bankruptcies, led to swelling unemployment. As a corollary, a new stratum of urban poor emerged which required new forms of relief and support. In the social backdrop was a demographic time-bomb. China was ageing rapidly, which was translated into rising costs for pensions and healthcare. The situation was aggravated by family change. In particular, the one-child policy not only raised the age dependency ratio but also made familycare of elders much harder to achieve. In the worst case scenario, a single child faces the prospect of tending both parents and four grandparents.

Transformation of the 'old' welfare system

The crowning feature of China's socialist welfare system can be captured by the phrase 'one country, many systems'. In specific terms, the total system consists of at least three components: a generous work-based welfare system for the urban population, a skeletal local self-help network for the peasantry, and a mean and stigmatized structure of relief and service support for designated needy groups and people without work and family. The three structures are remarkably different. The urban welfare system, composed of comprehensive social insurance and welfare amenities provided at the work place, compares favourably with provisions in advanced welfare states. Rural welfare is vastly inferior. Under the old collective framework, it nevertheless guaranteed a basic minimum in terms of nutrition, health and education. The lowest rung, aid to the destitute, suffers perennially from paucity of resources and marginality. When the three structures are compared, only the first tier can boast any claim to the 'superiority of socialism', albeit covering less than one quarter of the population.

In the context of open door and reform, social policy adjustments generally followed one step, if not a few paces, behind structural reform. In the new rural economy, welfare reform was heralded by attempts to re-construct a system of relief for homeless elders and orphans in the early 1980s, followed closely by the introduction of development loans to poor farmers, and finally by the promulgation of pension funds for peasant workers in the following decade.

As far as urban developments were concerned, a number of strands were important. Starting from the early 1980s, a number of coastal regions such as Guangdong, the special economic zones and Shanghai have begun to experiment with new pension plans, and 1986 saw a number of landmark changes in the labour field. These included the introduction of labour contracts for new recruits into state-owned enterprises, permission for open and competitive recruitment, legitimizing dismissal of recalcitrant workers, and introduction of unemployment insurance. Social insurance reforms, which are very important complements to enterprise restructuring, did not really take off until the state finally bit the bullet by allowing more firms to go bankrupt and to lay off workers on a large scale. This stage was reached in the early 1990s. Pension reforms were stepped up in 1991. Unemployment insurance was revamped in 1993. Pilot health insurance reforms were tested in various cities (for example, Shenzhen, Shanghai, Jiujiang and Zhenjiang) in quick succession. In the last few years, some enterprises have started to transfer occupational services to neighbourhood agencies or to run them with reduced resources or on fee-charging lines.

In the field of urban welfare and relief, state welfare agencies started to open their doors to fee-paying clients in the early to mid-1980s. At the same time, work schemes for the disabled were greatly expanded. From 1987 onwards, the Ministry of Civil Affairs put a lot of effort into promoting social services run by street offices and residents committees. Officially known as 'community services' (*shequ fuwu*), neighbourhood programmes are run on local funding and manpower. At the same time, the management of welfare institutions was also improved by stepping up training and establishing better staff mixes. When the unemployment tide began in earnest after 1994, urban relief was given a boost by expanding it to cover targets formerly excluded from aid, such as redundant workers, people with insufficient income and poor pensioners. In trying out pilot reforms, more advanced cities, such as Shanghai, Beijing, Wuhan and Guangzhou, have taken the lead while inland provinces are followers. This is understandable as the former have more resources for welfare development. They are also more open to exchange and learning from new practices and advice from international agencies such as the World Bank, International Labour Organization (ILO) and World Health Organization (WHO).

Two decades of social policy reform have produced substantial shifts from the Maoist mode. A number of features mark the post-reform paradigm of social policy.

First, efficiency replaced equality as the primary goal of social distribution. There are sundry empirical examples: the use of bonuses and piece rates, tolerance of unemployment and bankruptcies, cost containment in social security, and the fostering of markets in labour, housing, health and, to a lesser extent, education. There has also been greater tolerance of individual and regional income inequality. Meanwhile the state was conscious of the dangers of forsaking inequality. To mitigate the effects of extreme disparity and hardship, social policy was given the key task of sustaining social stability.

The state renounced its role of giving comprehensive guarantees of people's livelihood. The wish to reduce state meddling stood out clearly in the spread of household farm contracting and increasing firms' autonomy over recruitment, dismissal and welfare. More important is the policy to 'socialize social welfare', aimed at a wider sharing of involvement in administration and financing in health, education, housing and welfare. Delegating power to lower-level units eased the burden of the state. It was also seen as a better way to meet needs more flexibly and appropriately.

In terms of policy orientation, there was a clear shift towards devolution. After the demise of communes, peasants' autonomy in economic decision making was restored. Likewise, firms gained greater say in their operations, staffing and remuneration. In the meantime, the policy bias in favour of the urban areas remains as strong as ever, if not stronger, because of declining state investment in agriculture. Pampered treatment of the industrial elite has continued. More and more, however, the financial health of firms has emerged as the key factor in determining pay and welfare.

Changes were also made in organization and style of management. First there were moves to devolve social responsibilities from the central government to local governments, communities and social units. Second, instead of using direct intervention, the state now encourages individual effort and denounces dependency. Third, commodification of major social services has become more common. Adoption of service charges has spread more widely. Finally, service units of all types were expected to rely less on state grants and become more adept at earning revenue. The marketization strategy, however, has been a double-edged sword. On the positive side, there are gains in the range and quantity of services as well as improvements in quality. But the downside is that the less well-endowed – for example, the poor, backward areas and less efficient enterprises – suffer discrimination.

The welfare reform agenda

There have been many attempts to classify the diverse and complex strands in the country's welfare system. This is necessary because many ministries and social bodies contribute to the effort. The latest, and no doubt the most authoritative, attempt was made in 1994, at the Third Plenary Session of the 14th Party Congress. Under the new categorization, the country's welfare system (officially known as the social security system) has six components: social insurance, social relief, social welfare, preferential treatment (for soldiers and veterans), mutual aid and personal savings (*Zhongguo Shehui Gongzuo*, 1996, 4, p.6). The last two programmes are new additions to the established lexicon. To a greater or lesser extent, all programmes entailed redefining the role of the state and civil society. Due to space limitations as well as insufficient data, veteran welfare and private savings will not be explored here. The discussion that follows examines the developments in four programmes: namely, social insurance, social relief, social welfare and mutual aid.

Re-inventing social insurance

The heavy social burden borne by state and collective firms was a significant cause underlying their failure to compete with the non-state sector. From 1969 to the late 1990s, social insurance costs have been borne by each work unit individually after the agencies which had responsibility for administering social security (namely, the Ministry of Labour and trade unions) ceased to operate. This changed the essential character of the programme from a pooled scheme to a firm-based benefit. Under the new market economy, firms that have a surfeit of retired workers become vulnerable and severely disadvantaged *vis-à-vis* firms that have a younger workforce and lighter staff costs. Not surprisingly many state and collective firms are in this predicament. Some insolvent units cannot pay out wages, much less pensions, health and other social insurance benefits (Feng, 1996; Li, 1996; Wong and Ngok,

1997). The need to shift the responsibility for social insurance from enterprises to society is imperative.

Objectives of reform

The intention of social insurance reform is to produce a truly 'social-ized' system as opposed to a work-based programme. This will not only give relief to enterprises, but will also protect workers by anchoring its provision in a territory-wide administration, usually at city or county level. More importantly, this will abet labour mobility when the work-force is no longer tied down by firm-based benefits. There are at least four objectives in revamping social insurance (formerly called labour insurance). First, there should be multiple funding sources rather than sole reliance on enterprise funding so as not to deplete enterprise assets. While employers will continue to bear the bulk of the expendi-ture, employees have a duty to contribute to their own protection. Meanwhile, input from the state will only be indirect and in the form of tax exemptions. Second, there should be local pooling of collection and distribution to even out the risks across corporate and individual subscribers. This is vital in laying the foundations for market competition so that different types of enterprise can compete on an equal footing. Third, a modern social insurance system should compensate for all major forms of income risks including retirement, occupational injury, health, unemployment and maternity. Fourth, the system should, in the long run, be unified. This implies a centralized management struc-ture. In the future, entitlement would be made universal, correcting the present exclusions and equalizing social rights across the employed population in urban areas.

Achievements

What have been the achievements so far? On building a comprehen-sive social insurance system, the first four schemes have taken shape incrementally, beginning with pensions, then unemployment, and later work injury and health insurance. A small beginning was also made with maternity insurance for female employees. On funding diversification, the principle of employee contribution has been applied to retirement and unemployment insurance, but not for work injury and health schemes, which remain the responsibility of employ-ers. Workers now have to pay 3 per cent of their wages to their pension fund. In respect of unemployment insurance, introduced in 1986, employer subscription was initially 1 per cent of the basic wage, later changed to 0.6 per cent of actual income in 1993. This change is sensible since the proportion of basic wage (*biaojun gongzi*) makes up less than half of total take-home pay so that basing levies on work income (*gongzuo shouru*) is more appropriate. From 1998 onwards, employees started to pay 1 per cent of their wages towards unemployment insurance while employers paid 2 per cent of the wage bill. For healthcare, the work unit or *danwei* used to pick up the full treatment costs for staff and 50 per cent for dependants. In the event of waste and sharp cost inflation, however, managers have been forced to economize. Many *danwei* now designate where medical care can be obtained and limit the type of drugs and treatments that are covered. Employee co-payment is routinely demanded in an effort to cut abuse and instil user-responsibility. Now most insured workers have to make partial payments, usually 20 per cent. Some units even replaced reimbursements with a fixed monthly allowance, the amount varying with length of employment. Workers can pocket the sum if no consultation is needed but have to bear any excess costs incurred, barring treatment for major illnesses when they can negotiate with their *danwei* on how the bill should be split.

Steady progress has also been made on unifying funding and distribution of social insurance. Pooled insurance funds are now common, mostly at the municipal and county level. At the end of 1996, 88 million workers (78 per cent of workers who qualify for coverage) and 24 million retirees (95 per cent who qualify) were covered by the basic pension. Pension fund reserves amounted to 58 billion yuan (Hu, 1998, p.265). Relating to unemployment protection, 89 million workers qualified for unemployment insurance. Additionally, 31 million workers were covered by work injury insurance, 20 million were protected by maternity insurance and 8 million employees subscribed to insurance covering major illnesses (*Jingji Yu Xinxi*, 1997, 11, p.61). The latest health initiative, announced at the end of 1998, was a basic health insurance plan covering all urban employees and contributed to jointly by employers (paying 6 per cent of wages) and workers (paying 2 per cent) (*Renmin Ribao*, 7 December 1998).

Outstanding problems

The above achievements notwithstanding, a number of problems remain. First, with the exception of pension pools and unemployment insurance, up to 1998 most insurance schemes had not been 'socialized' to a significant extent. Instituting a partially funded system on the existing pay-as-you-earn mode may be useful in saving money in the longer term, such as, for instance, amassing surpluses to prepare for the old-age dependency crisis which is expected to peak in 2025. However, as a consequence of high inflation and conservative investment policies (only deposits in banks and purchase of state bonds are allowed), insurance funds fall prey to erosion. The risks resulting from depreciation and poor management make citizens wary of putting money in state programmes with a distant maturity date. In addition, fund surpluses have been rather modest, as has been the coverage of most types of insurance. Groups other than those working in state-owned and collective-owned enterprises can only join voluntary or commercial schemes. Even for those joining state plans, it is important to note that 'coverage' does not mean 'actual beneficiary'. The case of unemployment benefit is instructive. In 1996, only 3.3 million people out of a total of 5.5 million registered unemployed received unemployment relief, while the 9 million informally laid-off staff were excluded. In addition, benefit levels are too low to provide for a decent living standard under high inflation. In some places, unemployment funds have already been used up. Many firms are falling behind with their payments. All in all, unemployment insurance has not been the panacea it was hoped.

More importantly, the social insurance expenditure of enterprises has not diminished despite funding reforms. Healthcare costs, for instance, defy containment, economy drives notwithstanding. The main reason is inadequate funding of clinics and hospitals by the health authorities. Very often, state subsidies cover less than 40 per cent of recurrent costs, and treatment units are asked to become self-sufficient. The expected outcome is escalation of the health bill, which work units and insurers are unable to control. Employers' contributions to various types of social insurance are high. The *danwei* typically contributes 20 per cent of wages to staff pensions, 11–14 per cent of wages to health insurance, 0.5–1.5 per cent of wages to work injury and 0.8–1 per cent of wages to unemployment insurance (raised to 2 per cent in 1998). Total subscriptions add up to 32–35 per cent of the entire wage bill. This load is hefty for profitable firms; for *danwei* in financial trouble, it is downright ruinous. Meanwhile, because pay levels are still low, employee contributions cannot go much higher. Help cannot be expected from the government either, which suffers from dire financial constraints. To date, it is still resisting calls to inject money into social insurance.

Finally, the lack of uniformity in protection has not been redressed. Entitlement is still tied to ownership type and employment status. The state is now determined to speed up the extension of pension coverage to employees in the non-state sector and ultimately achieve uniformity in system design, management, benefit standards and fund usage. This will not be easy given different starting points and the multiplicity of vested interests. Despite the government's efforts to produce a common pension plan for all, until 1998, eleven industrial sectors (electricity, petroleum, water conservancy, transport, coal mining, post and telecommunications, civil aviation, construction, banking, coloured metals and railways) operated their own retirement schemes. The striking thing about these agencies is that most are well-endowed. Preventing the centrifugal forces from torpedoing the basic scheme is a grave test of state will.

Administrative unification

Bureaucratic infighting and inconsistency has been an institutional hindrance holding back social insurance reforms. As early as the mid-1980s, there were calls to end the chaos. One specific proposal was the setting-up of a high-level coordinating committee. Another was the creation of a centralized social security ministry. Neither has borne fruit due to intense rivalry from competing bureaus. The ideological debate may at last be coming to an end. In April 1998, the government announced the birth of a new super organ, the Ministry of Labour and Social Security (MLSS), to take charge of all social security matters. After more than a decade of experimentation and drift, social security reform finally received the attention it deserved, at the Fifteenth National People's Congress in 1997. It was also meant to complement the reform of state enterprises after the state declared its resolve to turn around the state sector in three years by letting go of the small and medium-sized units and concentrating its energy on reviving the big and strategic ones.

  Whether the new organization will be effective in improving policy effectiveness and administration, only time can tell. From what is known, the new MLSS has amalgamated all the social security functions undertaken by the Ministry of Labour (which has jurisdiction for welfare and social security for workers), the Ministry of Personnel (for cadres and government workers), the Ministry of Civil Affairs (for old age pensions for rural peasants), the Ministry of Public Health (for health insurance), and the State Commission for Reform of the Economic System (for social security reform planning). For example, the Ministry of Civil Affairs (MCA) has already transferred some 20 cadres and 12 billion yuan of rural pension reserves (covering 81 million peasants in 1997) to the new ministry. The next step is to finalize its jurisdiction, organizational structure, staffing establishment and work plans (field interview, May 1998).

Expanding social relief in urban areas

Plugging the gap between social insurance and social relief

Until now, only people who had no work, no families and no means of livelihood (the 'three nos') qualified for social relief from state civil affairs agencies. Such stringency excluded the vast majority of needy people from getting help despite the worsening problems of unemployment and urban poverty. For instance, current employees (including millions of workers in firms which have suspended or reduced production), pensioners and redundant workers who have exhausted their unemployment benefit are barred from relief. In 1996, some 32 million residents in urban areas fell into poverty, including 11 million workers whose wages were cut or stopped, 5.5 million registered unemployed, social relief recipients and their dependants (Zhu, 1998, p.225). Even among the unemployed, the benefit is restricted to those who are formally laid off and have registered with the local labour agency; the much larger group of workers sent down from their work post (*xiagang gongren*) and early retirees are not eligible. These artificial gaps become increasingly anachronistic when people are vulnerable to income interruption for many reasons and are seriously in need of aid from a single safety net.

To extend help to urban dwellers who fall into poverty for whatever reasons, Shanghai became the first city to experiment with a city-wide social relief allowance in June 1993. Officially known as the 'subsistence protection line' (*zuidi shenghuo baozhang xian*), this benefit supplements income up to an officially defined subsistence standard. Other cities soon followed with their own expanded relief schemes and poverty measures. By mid-1997, 185 cities had introduced expanded social assistance for their registered residents.

New watershed

September 1997 marked a watershed in subsistence protection. The then Vice-Premier, Zhu Rongji, became personally concerned about the hardship hitting many urban families. A meeting involving all top party and state leaders was convened to discuss the problem. The upshot was the issue of a new decree, the 'State Council Circular on Building a Subsistence Protection System in All Cities', which set the deadline for implementation at the end of 1999 (*Zhongguo Minzheng*, March 1998, p.18). Following the intervention of Zhu, now Premier, the expansion of social relief became more than a ministerial programme and finally advanced to the top of the government agenda.

All municipalities, two-thirds of county-equivalent cities and one-third of county capitals had to introduce the income protection scheme before the end of 1998 (*Jingji Yu Xinxi*, 1998, 2, p.60). In May 1998, when I visited the MCA, a quantum leap of sorts was reported: 400 cities (out of 666) and 464 county capitals were operating such a programme, from fewer than 200 cities some eight months previously. The number of people receiving social relief leapt to 2.25 million (field interview, May 1998). This example demonstrates the utmost importance of the personal involvement of a top leader in the policy process. In Chinese politics, the presence or absence of a top-level sponsor and advocate is absolutely vital in pushing an issue up the decision-making agenda and speeding up subsequent policy enforcement. The MCA is a ministry with very little clout. Without the push from a powerful leader, the expansion of social relief is likely to take a tortuous course.

Funding issues

The funding of subsistence protection is still inadequately resolved. Two methods of funding have been adopted. One is to have the Treasury at city and district levels take up the onus of the expanded scheme by allocating additional funds to civil affairs departments; the other is to spread the load among different agencies, meaning that each agency relieves those needy people under its jurisdiction. For example, enterprises grant aid to their own employees, insolvent enterprises get help from their supervising bureau, social insurance bureaus relieve paid-up subscribers, trade unions help retired workers, and civil affairs departments assist the 'three nos' and so on. This second formula is easier to run and appears more feasible. However, financing remains chaotic and uncertain. There is no final guarantor should any party default. Enterprise funding is often impractical as it was firm insolvency that caused staff lay-offs and worker hardship in the first place. Now, most cities have come round to using the first model to fund the expanded assistance scheme. However, the poorer cities have difficulties paying for this programme. A question thus arises about the role of the central government when the locality is unable to carry the financial burden. So far a solution has not been found.

Reforming social welfare services

The guiding concept informing welfare services is 'socialization of social welfare'. What this means is that in welfare matters, people should eschew dependence on the state. Instead, all strata of society – local communities, mass organizations, work units, families and individuals – must be actively involved. According to the MCA, popular participation can take a number of forms. Citizens should take part in service provision and management, and should also share in the financing of services. Besides, citizens can serve as volunteers or engage in acts of mutual help. Finally, the scope of services should widen to meet social needs of the masses and not just the traditional clients. In short, joint effort and diversification should be the fundamental principles in administering welfare when needs are far too numerous for the state to tackle on its own (D. Zhang, 1990).

A number of initiatives have been taken to extend the scope for collective social involvement. In the countryside, rural collectives have always carried the major burden of communal aid. After the reform, they are expected to do more. Administrative village and township governments, as the first tier of rural administration, inherited the welfare mantle from production brigades and communes. At the instigation of the MCA, rural communities have taken steps to systematize the operation of relief and welfare. Instead of having the hamlet (natural village) as the unit of accounting, the current practice is to centralize collection of welfare tax at the higher administrative village/township level; people eligible for relief are paid from the common pool. The more capable localities have likewise expanded the scope of welfare programmes. By the end of 1996, 35 per cent of all villages/townships had set up their own 'rural social security networks', meaning one old-age home, one welfare factory for the disabled, one social security fund, and a levy pooling system in the locality (*Zhongguo Minzheng Tongji Nianjian*, 1997, p.176).

In city areas, extension of 'socialized' care is more impressive. Two major strategies have been adopted: one is to relax eligibility for services. Formerly confined to people without work and families and needy veterans, state-run institutions have been admitting self-paying residents (for example, pensioners who have no family or whose family cannot take care of them). The other way to reduce the pressure on the state is to exploit the self-servicing potential of urban neighbourhoods. Actively promoted by the MCA in 1987, community services (*shequ fuwu*) were defined as the key ingredient of mutual aid. Discussion of this initiative will follow in a separate section.

Over the last two decades, the balance of the state–society division of welfare responsibilities has changed substantially. Specifically there have been reductions in state provision, state funding and state regulation, which are key indicators of social service privatization in the West.

Reduction of state provision

Direct state input has always been of subsidiary importance in welfare provision. Under Deng, community-run programmes became more important and overtook state amenities in terms of the number of service units, beds and residents. In 1979, state-run homes accounted for 9 per cent of units, 32 per cent of capacity and 36 per cent of residents. In 1995, their share fell to 5 per cent of units, 18 per cent of beds and 18 per cent of inmates. Similar things are happening in the area of work schemes for the handicapped. In 1981, state-run welfare enterprises outnumbered society-run units by two to one and the total workforce by three times. By 1985, the pattern was reversed. State-run welfare factories made up 15 per cent of units, 33 per cent of total employees, 35 per cent of disabled workers and 37 per cent of added value. In 1995, the respective percentages declined even more steeply to 13, 17, 16 and 11 per cent (Wong, 1998).

In sum, the mix of state and non-state provision has changed radically since the reform. Before, state programmes, though not dominant, were quite significant; now, local communities are the major providers. It is important to point out that the eclipse of the state was not caused by change of ownership. As far as institutional care is concerned, no selling of public assets, service closure or contracting-out has taken place, although signs of exhaustion and stagnation were visible towards the end of the 1980s. Likewise, privately run homes are just beginning to emerge in a number of cities such as Guangzhou and Shanghai. In the future, the MCA does not envisage building any new welfare homes; rather, the preferred option is to transfer some state homes to social organizations and local communities. The case is slightly different for welfare enterprises. Because of low productivity and backwardness, many plants are facing deficits and are unlikely to survive. According to informal sources, many welfare factories have closed down. Those that are still struggling have to lay off their disabled workers. Needless to say, few private operators are interested in taking over these establishments. Employment prospects for disabled people appear rather gloomy when even the able-bodied have problems finding work.

Reduction in state funding

The post-reform funding approach can be summarized as the policy of using 'multiple levels, multiple channels and multiple means' of financing. State financing has been marked by a number of bold initiatives. First, control has been loosened over the use that can be made of disaster relief funding. Formerly, it could only be spent as grants to disaster victims. Since 1983 the government has allowed some of the funds to be diverted to loans to help poor households start a business or production project. The programme of 'development loans' (*fupin*) was rationalized as turning 'dead money' (grants) into 'live money' (loans) as money paid back could be used to help other poor households.

Second, the state popularized the use of the contract responsibility system in disaster relief budgeting. What this means is that local areas that take part in this scheme manage their budgets within pre-set limits. While they can keep any unspent portion, they give up the right to ask for extra money, except in the case of dire emergencies. From 1984 onwards, the MCA also withheld disaster relief grants from rural counties with annual per capita income over 400 yuan, so that central funding is restricted to the most needy areas.

A more profound change came in 1985 in the guise of an administrative note, 'The Ministry of Civil Affairs and Ministry of Finance Joint Circular Regarding Adjustment to Preferential Treatment and Relief Standards'. The gist of this decree was to confer autonomy in standard-setting and financing to local areas, with the central government only concerning itself with statutory grants to martyrs, disabled soldiers and incapacitated veterans in institutions (*Minzhengbu Zhengce Yanjuishi*, 1986, p.253). The message that stands out loud and clear is a hands-off approach to local programmes. Since 1985, local governments have had to foot their own welfare bill and calculate their supply to match local demand.

As far as collective funding is concerned, the masses have long shouldered aid to soldiers' families, poor households and childless elders out of the welfare funds of production brigades and teams. After de-collectivization, rural communities paid for the support of needy groups through special levies. Most village communities have now centralized the collection and use of levies at the township or village level.

Apart from state and collective funding, the government has stepped up the exploitation of new sources of income. Instead of reliance on meagre state grants, welfare homes and enterprises were urged to become more active in raising revenue. When grants from the state were short, greater self-sufficiency was the key to survival. It also made possible improvement of services, better food for inmates, and bonuses for staff. Two methods have been adopted: wider fee-charging and profit-making activities.

Liberalizing entry into state-run welfare institutions has resulted in a modified resident profile. In 1979, self-financed access to social welfare homes and children's homes was virtually impossible; by 1995, paying clients accounted for 30 per cent of all residents. At the end of 1997, 60 per cent of in-patients in civil affairs-run mental hospitals paid for their own treatment. In old-age homes, 30–40 per cent of the residents were fee-paying, as were all tenants in elderly housing schemes (*laoren gongyu*). Meanwhile children's homes saw less than 10 per cent of inmates paying their own fees (field interview, May 1998).

An interesting innovation was the launching of welfare lotteries in 1987 with the purpose of raising money for charity (35 per cent of proceeds earmarked for prizes, 15 per cent for administrative expenses, and 50 per cent for welfare projects). In 1993 and 1994, some cities introduced a new lottery modelled on Hong Kong's Mark Six betting. This proved so popular that they had to be banned in 1994 for fear of encouraging gambling.

In the days of the Cultural Revolution, China prided itself on its self-reliance in solving domestic problems. International aid was routinely declined, except from other socialist states. Since 1980, a fundamental change in attitude has occurred, concomitant with state resolve to strengthen economic ties with the West. Disaster relief aid from Western countries, overseas and Chinese communities has poured into China after major disasters.

Additionally, there has been a proliferation of special funds. Variously called mutual benefit funds, social security funds, social welfare funds or social insurance funds, these are special collections set up for specific welfare purposes. Such funds have multiple funding sources. Many incorporate a contributory element whereby individuals and households pay monthly premiums to build up their eligibility to borrow, withdraw money for a contingency, or draw a pension. Profitable enterprises or wealthy individuals are also pressed for donations. Civil affairs departments sometimes give start-up grants or help with administration costs. Some of these are insurance schemes, covering, for example, the loss of crops, houses or draught animals. Some also give temporary handouts to the destitute and disaster victims. In 1996, 189 840 funds were in operation. Among these, rural pension schemes had a membership of 66 million and reserves of 9950 million yuan; mutual aid funds accumulated reserves of 4790 million yuan (*Zhongguo Minzheng Tongji Nianjian*, 1997, pp.171–2).

To sum up the developments in welfare funding, three important trends can be detected. First, there has been a substantial degree of devolution from central to local government, and also to communities. Second, funding sources have been diversified, and clever means devised to earn money for service agencies. Third, the proliferation of fee-charging has transformed a hitherto closed system. More and more, ability to pay has become a potent means to negotiate service access. Fourth, the chase for profits makes Chinese welfare agencies unique among welfare bureaucracies of the world. Of course, the state's role in welfare finance remains vital. Nevertheless, the proportion of welfare outlay in public expenditure has remained constant to an astonishing degree: during the course of the last five decades, civil affairs expenditure has stayed at 1.6 per cent of government spending (*Zhongguo Minzheng Tongji Nianjian*, various years).

Reduction in state regulation

Deregulation in social welfare took three forms. First, there was a clear move toward deregulation. Through new budget contracts and the 1985 decree, the central government has relinquished primary responsibility to local authorities and neighbourhood agencies. While the MCA has the power to set national policies, agencies on the ground take care of delivery. The second dimension was the liberalization of service access. The open door and fee-for-service policies meant that receipt of service no longer depended solely on designated status. The third means was the introduction of competition. Where there had been state domination in urban welfare provision, more players entered the field. Now, voluntary agencies, including religious bodies and organizations with overseas links, are allowed to run social programmes. International agencies have also set up operations in the last few years.

The growth of new social agencies, apart from the official 'mass organizations' such as the trade unions, Women's Federation and the Communist Youth League signals reduced state control on civil society. Under a more relaxed political climate, many organizations have thrived. Among the new crop are agencies in the fields of social work and social welfare. These can be classified into the semi-independent and independent categories (Y. Sun, 1995). Examples of the first variety are the China Disabled Persons' Federation, China Social Workers' Association, China Youth Development Foundation and the Association of Young Chinese Volunteers. Nearly all of them are instigated by the state and maintain close links with certain state bureaus. The second type of agency is not affiliated to the state. Notable examples are the Amity Foundation, and the Young Men's, and Women's, Christian Associations. These are often started by famous personages, local leaders and groups of like-minded citizens acting out of an urge to tackle a social problem. Invariably they are responsible for their own funding and policy making.

Compared to local agencies, international organizations are better placed to offer expertise and resources to the central and local state. Examples are numerous. UN agencies, such as the World Bank, United Nations Development Programme (UNDP), United Nations Children's Fund (UNICEF) and United Nations Population Fund (UNFPA), have been prominent in piloting poverty alleviation and integrated development projects.

The World Health Organization (WHO) has given assistance in the training of medical and rehabilitation personnel. Many countries have offered technical assistance and development loans. Among the non-local welfare organizations, those from Hong Kong have been particularly active in promoting social work training, running demonstration projects, and offering professional advice and guidance. Such links deepened and widened even before the 1997 change of sovereignty, and now look set to grow further.

Mutual aid

Mutual aid has always been at the heart of China's welfare enterprise. Rural communities and urban neighbourhoods are important vehicles of local solidarity and common welfare. During the last decade, the development of community care in urban neighbourhoods and philanthropy has gained increasing prominence. Under strong backing from the state, these two approaches support the new approach to mutual help.

Urban community services

Community services, or *shequ fuwu*, have been hailed as the new growth point in urban welfare. Thanks to the indefatigable efforts of the MCA, urban neighbourhood programmes sprouted rapidly. In 1988, community services were delivered from 69 700 service points across Chinese cities. At the end of 1996, there were 127 000 social service facilities and 259 000 service outlets offering housework, repair and livelihood services (called convenience services, or *bianmin fuwu*) to local residents (*Zhongguo Minzheng Tongji Nianjian*, 1997, p.172). Without exception, such services are run and funded by street offices and residents' committees.

Despite their heady growth, the nature and proper role of community services was at the centre of controversy in the 1990s. When the movement began, the core programmes consisted of welfare support for needy elderly, disabled, children and veterans at no charge. Gradually,

as neighbourhood agencies felt the pinch from local resource constraints and lack of government aid, the desire to branch out into running profit-making services became impossible to resist. Most of the
so-called convenience services, such as small shops, repair businesses,
karaoke bars, restaurants and so on bear little resemblance to a social
service, yet these have become vital to the survival of the money-losing
operations. In theory, the MCA requires 40 per cent of the earnings to
go towards the support of free services (field interview, May 1998). In
practice, observance is questionable. Indeed, many neighbourhoods are
losing interest in running free services while fee-charging amenities
have become unaffordable to the poor. Opinions now divide sharply
on whether commercial activities should be glorified as community
services (*Zhongguo Shehui Gongzuo*, 1997, 6, pp.38–9; 1998, 1, pp.37–8).
Calls on the government to offer regular resources to community programmes have come from many quarters, including some cadres in the
welfare ministry.

Philanthropy

The establishment of the China Charity Federation (CCF, or *Zhonghua
Cishan Zhonghui*) in 1994 is a significant milestone in harnessing the
potential of philanthropy. Interestingly, the CCF was started by the former Minister of Civil Affairs, Cui Naifu, the Vice-Minister, Yan Mingfu,
and other retired MCA officials. Designed to be the largest national
comprehensive charity organization approved by the Chinese government, the agency styled itself after the United Way in the United States
and the Community Chest in Hong Kong. Government support for its
creation reflects the realization that state effort alone can never meet
needs adequately and that vigorous tapping of donations from society
at large is essential. It also symbolizes a major value reversal. *Cishan*, or
charity, used to be abhorred; it was taken to mean almsgiving, class
patronage, social control, and imperialism (in the case of overseas missions). Now philanthropy is openly embraced by the state. Over the
years, most provinces have set up local branches of charity organizations, the largest of which is Shanghai's (field interview, May 1998).

Welfare socialization or privatization?

In the West, the retreat of state management of the economy and public services has been referred to as privatization, an emerging trend
since the 1970s. Reflecting a rethinking and redrawing of state–civil
society relationships, the impetus came from political aversion to the

ongoing viability and appropriateness of large-scale state intervention in public life. The more prominent concerns centre on the slowdown of economic growth, uncontrollable public budgets, inefficient state industries and public services, and insatiable social demands.

In the social services, privatization need not mean de-nationalization. It can be understood in a general sense as the rolling-back of state activities. According to Le Grand and Robinson (1984), this can happen in three ways: namely, through reduction in state provision, reduction in state funding, and reduction in state regulation. The UK offers a textbook case. Where public provision is concerned, the record consists of a programme of the sale of council houses, closure of local authority residential homes, expansion of private medicine, contracting-out of hospital cleaning and catering, use of education vouchers, and promotion of private health insurance and charity. In financing, cuts have been made in subsidies to remaining council housing tenants, charges have been introduced for services under the National Health Service, grants have been replaced by loans to university students, and subsidies have been lowered for public transport. Finally, examples of deregulation can be found in the easing of rent controls and the use of quasi-markets whereby large chunks of state services are now carried out by newly created public 'agencies', voluntary bodies and private contractors alongside traditional government departments (Hills, 1990; Johnson, 1990; Mishra, 1990).

The state can use a number of means to shed its welfare functions. Oyen distinguished at least five ways of trimming state social provision: (a) use of proprietary services; (b) subventing voluntary agencies to produce services instead of direct state provision; (c) fee-charging; (d) de-institutionalization and wider use of family, community, and informal care; and (e) curtailing national economic management and returning nation-wide programmes to local communities (Oyen, 1986). To varying extents, these strategies found common acceptance across Western Europe in the 1980s. In Eastern Europe, privatization of social care has taken hold to a large extent (Deacon and Szalai, 1990; Deacon, 1993).

The Chinese approach to welfare socialization

The Chinese use of the word 'socialization' has a different meaning from the conventional Western understanding. In the West, people equate socialization with nationalization. State-run medicine is often referred to as 'socialized medicine'. 'To socialize' has the meaning of taking assets into public ownership and operation: for example, the 'nationalization' of public utilities and strategic industries by the state. Indeed, in the early period, even the Chinese Communists adopted similar language. For example, the phase of nationalizing private trade and industry (1953–56) was known as the period of *shehui zhuyi gaizao* (socialist transformation). In a similar vein, public ownership is taken as the very essence of a socialist economy.

The meaning of 'socialization' appeared to have changed in subtle ways in the 1990s, especially as it pertains to the change of state welfare functions. Starting from the mid-1980s, 'socialization of welfare' crept into official use. During the course of the next ten years, *shehuihua*, or 'socialization', has been used more and more by officials across different ministries. In the last few years, even ordinary people have begun to embrace the new discourse. Nowadays, reforms such as the leasing of enterprise canteens to be run by private operators, the hiving-off of university car pools, and the transfer of state-run and enterprise-run welfare facilities to neighbourhood agencies and independent agencies are known as 'socialization'. Indeed, in the welfare field, the socialization policy has become a creed.

I believe that I am the first social scientist to point out the similarities between Chinese-style welfare 'socialization' and 'privatization' (Wong, 1994). To Chinese socialists, this suggestion may sound like heresy. In the eyes of Chinese leaders and academics, 'privatization' (*siyinghua* or *siyouhua*) is politically suspect. 'Private' suggests selfishness and disregard for the public good. 'To privatize' hints at capitalism and bourgeois liberalization, and for the state to do this implies an abdication of public duty. Given these perceptions, 'privatization' has not found its way into the official lexicon. Where a similar approach has been followed, as in market housing, unsubsidized flats are called commodity housing (*shangpin fang*). Similarly, the authorities are more tolerant of private medicine, private schools and private labour markets, and allow them to be called as such. Meanwhile the state makes no bones about the need for enterprises and public agencies to follow market demands, improve operational efficiency, confront competition, forgo dependence on the state, and charge fees for services. In short, there is ready acceptance of referents such as 'marketization' (*shichanghua*) or 'commodification' (*shangpinhua*).

Semantics apart, China's actual experience of socializing welfare has revealed a remarkable resemblance to privatization as it is known in the West. Under the reform and open door policy, greater pluralism in welfare has undoubtedly evolved. From the above review, it is clear that whether in provision, financing or regulation, there are clear moves to limit the scope of state activities and increase the demands on civil society. As far as actual policies are concerned, the Chinese government has tacitly accepted devolution. Furthermore, it has openly advocated fee-charging, community and informal care, and reforms in funding and management. To date, there are few proprietary programmes, and neither has there been a wide use of subvention to replace direct state provision. From the vantage point of civil society, the new tolerance of the activities by autonomous social agencies, in addition to state-controlled mass organizations, is a welcome change. Under this more tolerant climate, voluntary agencies of different hues become the purveyors of new approaches and professionalism (*China Development Briefing*, various issues; *South China Morning Post*, 28 April 1996).

The retreat of the state from welfare services is all the more remarkable in the context of state socialism. In Western welfare states undergoing privatization, the passing of state programmes to private agents involves a trading of responsibilities between two already existing sectors. More often than not, the state retains a funding role while ceasing to provide services directly. In essence, then, the change involves a transformation of the state role from 'provision' to 'enabling' and 'steering'. In China, on the other hand, the state has been the guarantor of living standards and social rights for more than 30 years. Shrinking state involvement stands in sharp relief against the ethos and structural arrangements of the old system. For these reasons, Chinese-style privatization may be more radical than market experiments under welfare capitalism. In the absence of state guarantees, the integrity of the social floor is in danger when duties borne by the state are not picked up by individuals and civil society. The social costs can be more serious than in societies with greater resources and administrative capability, and the cultural values that underpin welfare pluralism.

The nature of social insurance reform is more difficult to depict. Social insurance schemes are mandatory programmes run by state agencies. Still, the underlying rationale of social security reform is a renegotiation of the relationship between the employee, work unit and the state where previously the labour relationship was dualistic: that is, between the state (as represented by the work unit which acted as the agent of the state) and the individual labourer. In another sense, the overlap between the state and enterprises and between enterprises and employees was fused, with the dominant actor in the dyad assuming total responsibility for the other. This institutionalized dependency was found to be incompatible with market competition and efficiency.

It was especially bad for labour mobility. To loosen state–enterprise relations, more autonomy and role specificity for firms has come about by way of greater devolution of powers to managers, and the policy of substituting bank loans for direct state allocation as the main source of firm capital since 1985. The same thinking lies behind the reform of social insurance. In building new funding regimes, the state requires firms to pay their dues, and employees to shoulder their share directly. This will not only increase revenue but also pluralize involvement. More importantly, apart from managing the insurance plans, the state dissociates itself from taking on the burden of fund injection. Thus, in place of a unitary model of provision and financing, a 'socialized' model of social insurance amplifies the principle of distributing responsibility between enterprises and workers, while at the same time entrusting management matters to state agencies. In the last few years, commercial insurance has also made significant inroads among the more prosperous cross-section of the population. State-owned insurance companies even compete for business with labour bureaus and civil affairs agencies for such things as life assurance and pension plans. Even overseas insurers, such as American International Assurance Company (AIA), have gained permission to operate in China. The market for commercial insurance is expected to grow when China joins the World Trade Organization (WTO).

The Chinese are still uneasy about the term 'privatization'. In the West, 'private' is linked to the idea of autonomy, the third sphere, and actions pursued by individuals and groups outside state influence. This may explain why the party state is so worried: it feels it may be losing its hold on civil society. In the Chinese experience, few welfare programmes are run by market providers. Thus the moot point centres on the nature of service agents, as alternative funders and providers are not self-seeking individuals but communal agencies, such as street offices and residents' committees. The involvement of community groups is a manifestation of the ethic of altruism and mutual aid. The formal incorporation of community services, volunteering, philanthropy and voluntary agencies in the programme of mutual aid underscores such thinking. Consequently, 'non-state' is not the same as 'private', and 'socialization' is deemed more accurate in describing the shuffling of welfare duties.

Mainland officials and researchers are at home with the terms *minyinghua* (society or people-run activities) and *shangpinhua* (commodification of services). Different forms of mixed state–society involvement – *minban gongzhu* (people-run with public support/funding) and *gongban minzhu* (state-run with support from the masses) – are considered desirable. In the future, the authorities are prepared to foster the growth of more intermediary organizations (*zhongjie tuanti*). This is certainly the stance of the MCA. Where previously the emphasis of welfare socialization has been on diversification of funding, the latest emphasis is on multiplicity of provision and management through transferring service delivery to the non-state sector (*Zhongguo Minzheng*, July 1997, pp.23–5, December 1997, pp.31–2; *Zhongguo Shehui Gongzuo*, 1998, 1, p.16). My interviews with officials in the MCA in Beijing and the Shanghai Civil Affairs Department (in May 1998) have confirmed this preference. The pressing need from now on is to speed up the growth of intermediary organizations through the promulgation of policies and regulations, incentives, subvention rules and professional support. A more indirect role for the state – in policy making, rule-setting, regulation, standard-laying, support and guidance – is defined as the cornerstone of welfare socialization in the new millennium.

Relevance of global experience

To say that China has built up a welfare system with distinct Chinese characteristics in no way implies the irrelevance of global experience. To begin with, market reforms were not invented by China; they were inspired by experiments with market socialism undertaken by Hungary and other Eastern European states in the 1960s. China's social policy reform under Deng is in turn embedded in the structural transformation of the economy under a leadership anxious to modernize the country by reintegrating itself with the world economy after three decades of isolation. With increasing exposure to outside influences and conscious learning, its welfare reform agenda in many ways converges with international practices popularized in the last two decades.

In refashioning the social insurance system, China has engaged in wide-ranging research, including fact-finding missions overseas to as many as 20 countries (Yue, 1997). Specifically the new pension system bears the imprint of the multi-pillar model recommended by the World Bank, which has advised the Chinese government and found favour with the reform-minded State Commission for Restructuring the Economic System (White, 1998). The influence of Chile and Singapore is also relevant; the individual account concept is borrowed from Singapore's Central Provident Fund. Among international agencies that have offered advice to China, the part played by the Bank has been prominent. Their recent reports include *China: Pension System Reform* (1996) and *China 2020* (1997a) which, *inter alia*, study and make recommendations on pensions, healthcare and income distribution. China is very conscious of learning from the advanced practice of other countries. She is especially wary of what she construes as the negative examples (what Gordon White calls 'negative occidentalism') of highly generous and universal social insurance schemes in Western Europe and Scandinavia. In general, China's learning from abroad has been careful (China takes the initiative) and selective (China decides on where to learn, what to borrow and how to adapt). Great caution is practised in order to design a new system that meets the special needs of China as a low-income country with its massive population, policy and practice fragmentation, rapidly ageing population, relatively undeveloped finance markets and weak management capability.

In the area of welfare and relief, international agencies have left their mark too. The World Bank has been active in poverty alleviation in many rural counties. For example, its South-west Poverty Reduction Project is the biggest of its kind operated by an international agency in the country. Many rural projects incorporate elements of micro-lending, integrated development, poverty alleviation and indigenous training. Likewise, many international bodies have offered help and consultancy to the central and local state (*China Development Briefing*, various issues; Wong, 1998). China has also received considerable overseas financial assistance after major natural disasters. For example, the severe East China Floods in 1991 brought in donations in excess of 2.3 billion yuan.

Besides engaging in rural development work, foreign NGOs are deeply involved in promoting urban welfare projects such as service improvement and staff training in orphanages, the training of rehabilitation workers, technical assistance and facilities support to special schools, and the running of demonstration community projects. As mentioned above, the role of Hong Kong agencies is especially prominent.

Conclusion

Welfare policy reform in China has taken very specific forms in very specific circumstances. In the course of transition from plan to market, the old institutional arrangements were regarded as ill-suited to an economy devoted to the maximization of efficiency, economy and effectiveness. Out-dated notions of the old welfare regime must be dumped or reformed to serve the developmental tasks of the nation.

The above review has identified the contours of the reform process and commented on related issues. A constant theme has been the dynamic engagement with market forces in system re-engineering and innovation. This reform drive is subsumed under the framework of socialization. In revamping welfare, the party-state has pointed to consumer demands as new determinants of programme design and delivery. Likewise, the resources of civil society are to be used to the maximum extent possible, if only under the tutelage of the state. To Chinese reformers, the attraction of marketization and commodification lies in their promise to infuse life into rigid state services, promote efficiency and accountability, and enhance citizen choice. Chinese experience runs parallel to global thinking and practices in redefining the role of different sectors in social policy. In deciding to embrace the market in welfare reform, China is keen to reduce expectation on what she can deliver to her citizens. The constraints she faces in economic, political and institutional resources are obviously important in shaping this vision of a lean but effective state. Nevertheless, in weighing these against the supposed advantages of marketization, China runs the danger of neglecting key aspects of governance, namely that of legitimation and social protection, while inflating the potential of markets to help the weak and needy. Leaving citizens to swim in the tide of strong competition without a lifebuoy will increase instability and suffering. The spectre of massive social unrest is only too palpable as China enters the twenty-first century.

4
Health Policy Reform

Anthony B. L. Cheung

> China since the 1980s has been moving towards less govern-
> ment support for priority public health activities for all and
> clinical services for the poor, and greater reliance on a fee-for-
> service delivery system. If present trends persist, China will
> move into the 21st century with a poorly performing but
> nonetheless costly health system.
>
> (World Bank, 1977a, p.65).

This is the recent World Bank report on financing healthcare in China.
If such a worry, expressed by the normally pro-free-market World Bank,
is to be taken seriously, then the prospects for China's healthcare system are very much called into question.

China is not the only country which needs to rethink its healthcare
policy and restructure its health finance system. Throughout the
world, most nations are engaged in healthcare reform of some kind.
Ham (1997a, p.136), for example, has identified three distinct phases
of healthcare reform internationally since the 1970s (see Figure 4.1).

Each of these phases has ultimately been geared towards the containment of rising medical costs, particularly in hospital services. As Ham
observed, the shift from the integrated to the contract model was stim-
ulated by the move in the second half of the 1980s in OECD countries
to supplement policies to contain costs at the macro level with initiatives to increase efficiency and enhance responsiveness to users at the
micro level (Ham, 1997a, p.8).

On the surface healthcare reform in China seems to be moving in a
direction similar to that in other countries: that is, trying to lessen the
government's burden of providing heavily subsidized public healthcare
through introducing alternative funding arrangements and market-based

PHASE I (Late 1970s/early 1980s): THEME:	Cost containment at the macro level

POLICY INSTRUMENTS:	Prospective global budgets for hospitals
	Controls over hospital building and the
	  acquisition of medical equipment
	Limits on doctors' fees and incomes
	Restrictions on the numbers undertaking
	  education and training

PHASE II (Late 1980s/early 1990s): THEME:	Micro efficiency and responsiveness to users
POLICY INSTRUMENTS:	Marketlike mechanisms Management reforms Budgetary incentives
PHASE III (Late 1990s): THEME:	Rationing and priority setting
POLICY INSTRUMENTS:	Public health Primary care Managed care Health technology assessment Evidence based medicine

Figure 4.1   Phases of healthcare reform

Source: Ham (1997a), p.136.

initiatives. Some of the reform initiatives being tried out in China are similar in concept to the managed care systems adopted in some OECD countries to contain cost escalation.

It is tempting to consider China's reform in a 'privatization' perspective, given the country's economic reform since the late 1970s which substituted a market economy for the previous state-planning economy; and now a booming private sector is being nurtured inasmuch as SOEs are being converted into stock-holding companies and put on the open market under recent SOE reforms. Upon further examination, however, as this chapter argues, even economic reform in the Chinese context is not merely an *economic* issue of how to make the most efficient allocation and use of resources. Every reform has an important *social* dimension in the sense that the old state-planning system was supported by a socialist regime whereby an individual's social well being (welfare, education, employment, health, housing and even entertainment) was fully taken care of by the work unit (*danwei*) which more or less 'owned' the individual; workers could not move to work in another unit without their former unit's consent. Social policy reforms have been triggered by the economic system reform which gradually but steadily caused an erosion of the *danwei* regime. But precisely because of the reforms' social implications, they are shaped and constrained by such repercussions.

The pre-reform system

Features

The healthcare system in China prior to economic reform in the late 1970s can be characterized as one based on preventive rather than curative medicine, supported by state and enterprise insurance in the cities and some form of cooperative coverage in the countryside. Essentially there were three basic components of the system: (a) government-funded healthcare (*gongfei yiliao*) which covered state employees in the government, the military and other state institutions at all levels, funded directly by the state budget; (b) labour insurance healthcare (*laobao yiliao*) which applied to employees in state-owned enterprises and most of the collectively-owned enterprises, financed by the enterprises' specially designed welfare fund;[1] and (c) cooperative healthcare (*hezuo yiliao*) for the rural population, financed by collective funds and individual contributions. Table 4.1 summarizes the features of these three components of the health insurance system.

Table 4.1   Health insurance systems in China

	Urban		Rural
	Government-funded health insurance	*Labour health insurance*	*Cooperative healthcare*
Establishment time	1952	1951	During collectivization in the late 1950s
Beneficiaries	Government officials Employees in governmental institutes Disabled veterans College students	Employees in state-owned enterprises Some employees in collectively-owned enterprises	Farmers
Coverage	32 million	120 million	100 million
Source(s) of Funding	State budget	Welfare fund of enterprises	Mainly individual contributions, supplemented by collective funds
Expenditure in 1995	13.8 billion yuan	51.5 billion yuan	(Not available)

Source: R.H. Cai (1997); adapted.

It can be seen that state employees were the best insured part of the population in healthcare, followed by the urban working population. Hospitals were located mainly in the cities and major towns, and were owned and managed either by the Ministry of Health and its lower-tier health bureaus/departments, or by other state institutions such as the military, civil aviation, railway and some large state-owned enterprises. The rural farmers were subject to a system which was relatively less stable in terms of funding. However, in order to improve the situation, the government had in the past encouraged the setting-up of village clinics by rural collectives with some limited state funds. The introduction of 'barefoot doctors' (essentially village health workers equipped with some elementary medical training) in the 1960s, though giving rise to other problems during the excesses of the Cultural Revolution, had helped to bring cheap healthcare to the rural poor whose needs might not otherwise be met by the limited supply of college-trained urban doctors.[2]

Policy goals and achievements

Four major national health goals were set at the establishment of the People's Republic of China in 1949: namely 'facing the workers, peasants and soldiers'; being more 'prevention-oriented'; 'integrating Chinese and Western medicine'; and 'integrating healthcare work and mass movement' (Peng, Cai and Zhou, 1992, p.3). These goals were largely achieved in the next few decades despite the instability and turmoil of the Cultural Revolution from the late 1960s onwards and the lack of adequate state finance in most hospitals. Achievements during the 1950s–70s were impressive. From a low starting point of an average life expectancy of only 32 in 1950 as estimated by the World Bank (1984), China managed significantly to improve its national health and to curb or eliminate most endemic and epidemic diseases. According to the Minister of Health (Chen, 1997), the infant mortality rate in 1997 was 31.4 per 1000, compared to 200 per 1000 before 1949. The mortality rate in pregnancy was lowered to 61.9 per 100 000 from 1500 per 100 000. Life expectancy had jumped to 70.8.

By 1975 urban insurance coverage (provided by the government and state enterprises) and the rural cooperative healthcare system reached close to 90 per cent of the population, which meant almost all of the urban population and 85 per cent of those living in the rural areas (World Bank, 1997a, p.1). Despite almost universal coverage and relatively good access to preventive and curative health services (by developing country standards), the cost of the system was low. In 1981 healthcare costs were just over 3 per cent of GDP (World Bank, 1997a, p.2). This performance can from any perspective be regarded as an out-standing success, especially considering the tremendous improvements made in such a huge country as China and within such a relatively short period of time.

Problems of funding

One of the outcomes of the state-planning regime set-up after the founding of the People's Republic was the rapid nationalization and collectivization of health personnel, as occurred also in other spheres of economic and social activities. Whereas in the early days of the repub-lic privately-employed health personnel formed the bulk of the med-ical profession, they had become almost non-existent during the Cultural Revolution (see Table 4.2).

Nationalization and collectivization meant that there was no longer any private or market sector in healthcare provision, and the popula-tion had to depend totally on state or collective services which had, however, suffered from a declining level of financial support.

After the First Five Year Plan (1953–57), health expenditure persis-tently declined as a proportion of total state expenditure. Since hospi-tals were directly financed by the state budget through their respective sponsoring institutions, their fees were kept at a nominal level; as a result, particularly when the state budget ran into fiscal difficulties, they were very often unable to accumulate enough revenue to meet operational expenses. Despite objections from the Ministry of Health, the government decided to drastically reduce healthcare fee levels

Table 4.2 Numbers of health personnel in various forms of employment, 1950s–1970s

	Privately-employed	*Collectively-owned health organizations*	*State-owned health organizations*
1950	488 000 (78.3%)	3000 (0.5%)	133 000 (21.2%)
1958	41 000 (2.7%)	854 000 (55.8%)	634 000 (41.5%)
Cultural revolution days	1900 (mainly traditional Chinese medicine)	About 20% of total health personnel population	About 80% of total health personnel population

Source: Peng *et al.* (1992), pp.4–5.

three times, resulting in such fees contributing only one-third to one-quarter of the costs (Peng, Cai and Zhou, 1992, p.5). The Cultural Revolution caused great damage to the economy and state finance, as well as serious disruptions to the overall healthcare management and funding systems, so that by 1976 the problems faced by the healthcare system were described as: 'hard to see a doctor, hard to enter a hospital, hard to have an operation'. There was a serious problem of underfinancing of healthcare from state resources. Under-investment due to the lack of adequate state and collective funding and unsatisfied demands from those in need of medical care were the main defects of the system. It can be argued that the underfunding of state hospitals and the nationalized/collectivized health personnel had helped to sustain a generally effective low-cost healthcare regime since the 1950s but, once such funding controls became relaxed after the 1970s, problems began to emerge.

The rural sector was the hardest hit in the new era. Before the advent of economic reforms in the late 1970s, the rural population of China did not enjoy any systematic health insurance schemes as these applied only to the urban workers. Some form of cooperative healthcare supported by village collective funds and individual contributions did exist, but was rendered almost redundant by the collapse of the rural commune system and the lifting of restrictions by the government on clinic fees and prescription charges. Village households have become the worst affected by the changing healthcare regime. According to Zheng (1997, p.335), only 10 per cent of the rural areas in China today still retain some form of cooperative healthcare. Of the 651 031 village-level health treatment points in 1993, private doctors comprised 44 per cent, while village/communal cooperative health points accounted for only 37 per cent and village clinics the remaining 19 per cent (quoted in Zheng, 1997, p.358). For the 700 million peasant population, nearly 90 per cent now pay out of their own pockets for almost all their health services. Publicly-run health institutions, now in receipt of minimal state subsidies, charge higher user fees even for emergency services (World Bank, 1997a, p.47). And as argued above, fee-for-service payment systems tend to push up health spending. It will also widen the inequity in access to essential healthcare because of the income disparity. Whereas in 1985 only 4 per cent of the rural population was reported to be unable to see any doctor when ill due to the lack of financial means, this percentage jumped to 7 per cent in 1993, with that in the poorest areas reaching as high as 72.6 per cent (Ministry of Health information, quoted in Zheng, 1997, p.360).

The reform programme

Directions and models

The present reform of China's healthcare system mainly took the form of healthcare finance reform which began to feature more prominently on the national policy agenda in the early 1990s when the government also attempted to 'commodify' educational, housing and healthcare benefits. Until then, these were all tied to the work unit of the employees as a kind of socialist occupational welfare, funded out of the state budget as explained above. In much the same way as the rural sector was the less organized and insured part of the previous healthcare system, current reform has also focused mostly on the urban population and enterprises.

Pilot reforms in Zhenjiang and Jiujiang

Pilot reforms in *Zhenjiang* and *Jiujiang* (the two *jiangs*), which started in late 1994, are the most significant in that their results have been officially recognized as providing a successful model for reforming the urban health insurance systems. Following a National Working Conference of Widening Pilot Spots for Employee Health Insurance System Reform in April 1996, jointly convened by the State Economic System Reform Commission, the Ministry of Finance, the Ministry of Labour and the Ministry of Health, the State Council decreed (see Document No. 16 of 1996) that all provincial governments should introduce employee medical insurance reforms on the basis of the two *jiang* experience.

Both Zhenjiang and Jiujiang are medium-sized cities with about 2.5 million population each. The experimental health insurance systems they have developed are essentially a kind of contributory scheme with mandated contributions from employers and employees. These contributions go into individual and social accounts (the latter being constituted as a Social Coordinating Fund) from which to draw to pay for medical fees (see Figure 4.2).

Health expenditures are funded through three tiers of financing. The first tier is the individual account. The second tier consists of out-of-pocket expenditures for medical fees which exceed the amount in an employee's individual account. The third tier is the Social Coordinating Fund which provides a kind of community risk-pooling mechanism, designed to insure workers against the financial burden of catastrophic illness, beyond what can be financed by their individual account and their out-of-pocket ability. In general, when a worker's

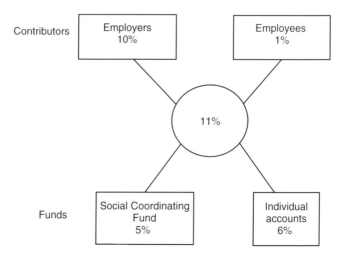

Figure 4.2   Wage contribution flows to individual and social accounts in the Jiujiang and Zhenjiang models

Source: World Bank (1997a), p.58, Figure 7.1.

healthcare payments exceed the balance in the individual account, the worker has to pay a deductible fee of 5 per cent of his or her annual wage income before receiving reimbursement from the social fund. In Jiujiang, the worker has to bear 15 per cent of that surplus payment if it is up to 5000 yuan, 9 per cent if between 5000 and 10 000 yuan, and 2 per cent if beyond 10 000 yuan. The corresponding payment ratios in Zhenjiang are 10, 8 and 2 per cent respectively (Zheng, 1997, pp.337–8).

In theory, the personal fund plus co-payment should help to keep patient demand moderate while the social fund provides coverage to protect against catastrophic medical bills. Other means, including an essential drugs list for the purpose of reimbursement (1100 Western and 500 traditional Chinese medicines), were introduced to help contain medical costs (World Bank, 1997a, p.58). A key feature of the two *jiang* model is the separation of funding and provision, similar to the separation of purchasing and provider functions in the healthcare reforms of other countries such as the UK (Ham, 1997b). The funding framework is broadly similar to the Singapore Medisave scheme which combines individual medical savings accounts with a community-wide insurance fund for major illnesses and conditions (Yuen and Yan, 1997).

Other reform models

In response to the 1996 State Council directive to expand healthcare insurance reform at the national level on the basis of the two *jiang* model, some 57 cities (such as Guangzhou, Dalian, Zhuhai, Xiamen, Ningbo and Weihai) have joined in the reform initiatives by combining individual accounts with community risk pooling. However, there are also other cities and provinces (notably Beijing, Chengdu, Shanghai, Shenzhen, Qingdao and Hainan Province) which prefer to adopt their own models, although along broadly similar conceptual lines of reform (Zheng, 1997, ch. 9).

In *Shenzhen*, the city government set up the Social Insurance Bureau and Health Insurance Bureau in August 1992 as part of the implementation of integrated provisional social insurance and health insurance schemes. Health insurance covers all employees of government, enterprise and social organizations, as well as retirees and unemployed workers who are receiving unemployment insurance support. There are three levels of basic insurance coverage.

First of all, there is *hospitalization insurance*, for migrant workers and the city's unemployed workers, funded by a social coordinating fund contributed to by employers and the unemployment insurance agency on the basis of 2 per cent of the average monthly wage income of the previous year; individual payment is not required. When receiving treatment, workers pay for all out-patient charges and receive 90 per cent support from the social coordinating fund for hospitalization expenses.

Integrated health insurance (comprising both hospital and out-patient care), for Shenzhen-registered workers and retirees, is funded by employer units and individual workers on the basis of 7 per cent and 2 per cent respectively of monthly wage income (retired workers being not required to contribute), and operated in the form of individual accounts and a social coordinating fund, as in the two *jiang* model. The individual account is made up of the employee's own contribution and 50–60 per cent of the employer's contribution after deduction of 2 per cent for management fees and 4 per cent for a risk reserve fund. The balance of the employer's contribution then goes into the social coordinating fund. The result is that there is a large individual account versus a relatively small community risk pooling fund. Workers basically pay for their own out-patient expenses (in certain circumstances, a portion of the expenses in excess of 10 per cent of the previous annual city average wage level can be met by the social coordinating fund), while the social fund pays for 90 per cent of hospitalization expenses (95 per cent for retired workers).

Finally *special health insurance* is targeted mainly at veterans who need not contribute or make any co-payment. Funding comes from the original work unit's budget.

In *Hainan Province*, the provincial people's congress passed special regulations in July 1995 to implement urban workers' health insurance reform. Although the insurance scheme features both a social account and an individual account, as in the two *jiang* model, the two accounts operate quite independently. Contributions are calculated on the basis of 10 per cent of monthly wage income by employers and 1 per cent by employees, with the self-employed contributing the whole 11 per cent. The individual account comprises the employee's contribution plus 40–60 per cent of the employer's contribution according to the employee's age. Two separate lists of reimbursable treatment types are maintained for payment purposes, by the individual and social accounts respectively. For social account treatment, workers have to bear 5–15 per cent (2.5–7.5 per cent for retired workers) of the expenses depending on how much such expenses have exceeded the social average monthly wage. For individual account treatment, workers pay for any expenses in excess of the reimbursable limits out of their own pockets.

The *Beijing* and *Chengdu* approaches are modelled on the Ministry of Labour's 1992 directive on providing social coordination for major treatment to workers in enterprises (the so-called '*dabing tongcho*') whereby no individual account is maintained and minor treatment is covered by the enterprises as in the traditional system. From April 1995 the whole of Beijing municipality implemented the new scheme under which enterprises and workers contribute respectively 6 per cent and 1 per cent of the city's average monthly wage to a municipal social coordinating fund. Chengdu has adopted since 1993 a tripartite contributory system comprising government, enterprise and employee contributions.

The *Qingdao* scheme (introduced in August 1995) consists of an individual account, an enterprise adjustment fund and a social coordinating fund, with the former two accounts managed by the enterprise and only the social fund managed by the city social insurance bureau. Employees and retirees pay for medical treatment out of the individual account and any excess amount is met by the enterprise adjustment fund (10–20 per cent of which is funded by employee contributions). For treatment costing more than the prescribed ceiling (presently 3000 yuan), part of it is covered by the social fund in a declining ratio of 90:80 per cent, with the balance borne by the individual and enterprise adjustment fund accounts.

In *Shanghai,* a three-phase approach to health insurance reform is adopted, beginning with an enterprise worker hospitalization insurance scheme, followed by an integrated social coordinating and individual accounts scheme, and finally achieving a fully societalized structure.

Village health finance reforms

Most of the reform initiatives in health insurance continue to focus on the relatively more privileged urban working population in the main cities. In some of the attempts to re-organize rural healthcare, attention was given to securing collective/social coordination for major illness (*dabing tongcho*). In 1989–90 the Ministry of Health, supported by the World Bank, spearheaded a Rural Health Insurance Experiment in Sichuan Province, involving a sample of 26 villages in two counties and 40 400 people (World Bank, 1997a, pp.49–50). Over 99 per cent of the rural population in the pilot rural townships and villages participated in a health cooperative insurance scheme which aimed to confine minor treatment within the village and major treatment within the township (*xiaobing buchucun, dabing buchuzhen*). Three insurance benefit plans were implemented with varying reimbursement rates for in-patient and out-patient services. Premiums were set at 1.5 per cent of average income, and insured peasants could freely visit village and township clinics but could visit county hospitals only in an emergency or with the approval of the township health centre (Word Bank, 1997a, p.50).

A WHO study of 14 Chinese counties in Beijing, Henan, Jiangsu, Zhejiang, Jiangxi, Hubei and Ningxia (Word Bank, 1997a) found that a typical community fund might collect 5 yuan per person from rural households, 1 yuan per person from the village's social welfare fund and 1 yuan per person from the township. Patients typically have to pay a deductible fee (for example, 100 yuan) and make a co-payment on expenditures above the deductible level. The schemes also set limits on coverage of drugs and reimbursement for diagnostic tests.

It can be seen that despite the variation in the details of funding and payment arrangements, all the reform models, whether urban or rural, have emphasized some form of co-responsibility between the individual and communal risk pooling (mainly through the individual account and the social coordinating fund). They all point towards the direction of a new notion of collective welfare known as *societalization,* in place of state direct responsibility to provide the final insurance coverage. The background to this change can be observed in the economic reform of the past two decades.

Reasons for change

The need for reform did not come directly from within the healthcare system despite the various problems of the previous system already identified in the last section. It was the transformation since the late 1970s of the Chinese economy gradually from a centrally-planned one into a competitive market system which ultimately provided the impetus for change.

Impact of economic transformation

In rural China, the advent of the household responsibility system and the subsequent demise of the communes after the Cultural Revolution virtually meant the collapse of communally-supported healthcare networks as the family re-emerged as the main organizing factor of village economic and social life. In the cities, resource-limited government units and inefficient state enterprises were finding it increasingly difficult to sustain the previous insurance coverage. Government/SOE sectors gradually gave way to the emergence of smaller private enterprises which, under the new economic climate, did not automatically take on the responsibility to provide healthcare insurance coverage for their workers.

In order to alleviate the fund-starved hospitals in times of rising costs and inflation during the economic reform era, the state allowed hospitals to introduce some form of commercialization as a means to supplement hospital income. User fees have since become increasingly relied upon to support hospital operations to the extent that a clear trend of marketization has set in, favouring the more affluent and definitely disadvantaging the rural and urban poor. There is also a growing emphasis on charging high fees for drugs as another means to create hospital income (so-called 'using drugs [income] to support the hospital' (*yiyao yangyi*). In Guangzhou, for example, where state appropriation to hospitals registered a steady and continuous decline from 5.75 per cent of the total budget of the municipality in 1981 to 2.85 per cent in 1991, hospitals had to introduce new categories of services, laboratory tests and prescriptions which were outside the normal government price-setting control, thus leading to the soaring of medical expenses (Lee, 1997, p.35). Apart from earning revenue from drugs-dispensing, hospitals also seek to encourage patients to accept more expensive curative services. As a result many unnecessary procedures are being performed; overprescription and inappropriate prescription are serious and widespread (G. Sun, 1992, p.60; Bo and Dong, 1993, p.58). A shift from the pre-1970s emphasis on preventive medicine to one more geared towards curative medicine is now clearly evident because of the new incentive system for healthcare providers to induce the consumption of more expensive hospital-based services under the 'fee-for-service' regime. Healthcare cost escalation at an annual rate in excess of 20 per cent was common for many Chinese cities during the 1980s (C.M. Zhou, 1995, pp.3–15). This tendency increases healthcare costs for society as a whole but, at the same time, reduces access to care because of the fee barrier, a phenomenon which is of increasing concern to national policy makers.

Collapse of the previous healthcare system

As Liu (1996, p.64) observed, as the economic reforms progressed, all three components of the previous healthcare system have undergone changes, with the countryside experiencing the most radical adjustment. Due to the collapse of the communes which had previously supported cooperative healthcare, by 1985–86 remnants of the cooperative system had survived in less than 5 per cent of the villages. After efforts during the subsequent years to re-establish village clinics, only 10 per cent of the villages had succeeded in doing so by the beginning of the 1990s. Village 'barefoot doctors' have now largely disappeared. For an overwhelming majority of the rural population, cash payments have become the only option to secure healthcare, and peasant families have essentially to rely on their own income to pay for the services.

As a result, the healthcare system has been biased even more towards the urban population than before economic reforms. In the early 1990s less than 15 per cent of China's population were covered by the government-funded and labour insurance healthcare systems, but this group utilized 44 per cent of the total health expenditure of the country (Liu, 1996, p.65). State enterprises and industries owned around one-quarter of all hospital beds and employed one-third of all health personnel, which served only one-tenth of the population (Peng *et al.*, 1992, p.57). The disparity of access to affordable healthcare between the rural and urban population was becoming alarming. In the urban areas, decline in state funding had meant inequity of another kind as higher income families were better able to 'buy' increasingly expensive medical services, whereas ordinary workers were being constrained by budget-limited labour insurance.

As Wong, Heady and Woo (1996) pointed out in an Asian Development Bank study of China's fiscal management system, the country suffered from the decline in government revenue (as a proportion of Gross National Product) and the resulting increase in the government budget deficit, as well as rising expenditure demands, against a background of difficulties and uncertainties in central–local fiscal relations which were affecting revenue mobilization. The social security expenditure (comprising welfare support, disaster relief, retirement insurance, medical insurance and unemployment insurance) of urban-based enterprises had increased from 14 per cent of the their total wage bill in 1978 to 27 per cent in 1987, an increase from 2 per cent to 5 per cent of GDP (Wong, Heady and Woo, 1996, p.13), triggering great concerns for controlling the upward cost trend. On the other hand, the unstable fiscal system had also caused the need to explore alternative ways of social funding of various social insurance schemes previously financed directly by the state budget. Enterprise reforms in the cities also meant that, in order to rationalize the cost structure of enterprises so as to re-establish efficiency and profitability, some previous *danwei* responsibilities (such as social insurance) would have to be given up.

Economic reform-inducing redefinition of collective welfare

While the commodification and privatization of the Chinese economy have unleashed great momentum for growth and other radical changes in society, they have at the same time rendered the previous healthcare finance and delivery systems virtually unsustainable, creating new problems of access, equity, efficiency and cost control. The problems facing reformers in China are how to provide a proper incentive system to health provider institutions and how to recreate an effective health finance system to support rising healthcare costs in light of the erosion, if not the collapse, of the state funding regime, so as to ensure there is reasonable access to healthcare for all. Depending entirely on the free operation of the market does not seem to be a solution because only the economically better-off are able to benefit from an increasingly user-fee-oriented system. As even the World Bank has admitted, '[h]ealth is a sector that cannot simply be left to market forces' (World Bank, 1997a, p.2).

China's healthcare system is facing dilemmas amidst rapid economic and social changes that see a steady decline in the role and capacity of the government and state enterprises. Collectivization and communalization are definitely a legacy of the past. There is no way for the system to revert to the previous regime. On the other hand, wholesale privatization of healthcare is not the answer either, as the reformers also recognize. Viewed within a broader context, those experiments tried out in reforming the urban health insurance systems (for example, in the two *jiangs*, Shenzhen and Shanghai) and in re-establishing community financing of some kind in the rural areas (for example, the Sichuan Rural Health Insurance Experiment) are in essence part of a larger attempt to re-accommodate social security systems within a changed environment driven more by market forces than government direct provision. As such, the direction of healthcare finance reform is towards a new form of *societalization* (*shehuihua* in Chinese) rather than *privatization per se*. The success of any such societalization regime (which incorporates some elements of privatization and commercialization) has to be appraised to establish how capable the new system will be of maintaining a cost-effective healthcare system which can still provide universal access and does not unduly widen the growing disparity among different sectors of the population (particularly between the urban affluent and the rural poor).

Impact and limitations of reforms

Improvements

As reforms have only just been implemented, on a still largely experimental and selective basis, their national impact has yet to be fully gauged. It was claimed that the pilot schemes in Zhenjiang and Jiujiang were instrumental in eliminating coverage gaps, which are particularly large among school teachers and workers in deficit-ridden enterprises, and in reducing the annual rate of growth in aggregate hospital expenditures, by 23–28 percentage points from the previous average annual rate of 33 per cent in 1991–94 (quoted in World Bank, 1997a, p.58). The rates of overprescription and use of expensive diagnostic tests were also cut significantly. Both in-patient and out-patient visits had declined for enrollees on the insurance plans. Tables 4.3 and 4.4 highlight the progress of the new schemes.

Transferability of the reform experience

The success in Zhenjiang and Jiujiang, however, does not necessarily mean that their model can be emulated easily by other cities in China. For one thing, the two *jiangs* are only medium-sized cities with relatively less complex demographic and social structures. Large municipalities, such as Shanghai, Beijing and Guangzhou, may face more problems in implementing the pilot model. Whereas Shanghai and Beijing opted to try out their own models, Guangzhou has decided to adopt the two *jiang* model but has encountered some inherent problems which make implementation difficult.

Table 4.3 Progress in the Zhenjiang and Jiujiang pilot experiments, 1995–96

	Zhenjiang		Jiujiang	
	1995	*1996*	*1995*	*1996*
Number of units qualified to participate	3 929		5 756	
Number of units covered	3 881		5 517	
%	98.8	97.3	95.9	96.1
Number of employees that should be covered	461 600		501 900	
Number of employees that have been covered	453 600		473 600	
%	98.3	96.4	94.4	94.7
Estimated amount of collectible health insurance funds (million yuan)	186.6		154.6	
Actual amount of health insurance funds collected (million yuan)	180.7		129.9	
%	96.9	95.9	84.0	90.1

Source: R.H. Cai (1997).

Guangzhou provides a good illustration of the limited transferability of the two *jiang* experience. It is an old city with an ageing population and a large percentage of retirees who cannot contribute to any insurance scheme but have to rely on the support of their previous work units to pay for medical services. Healthcare costs are high because of higher wages in Guangzhou and more advanced but expensive medical facilities. In the late 1980s, public health insurance payments increased

Table 4.4 The percentage of population in each segment of the total insured population in Zhenjiang and Jiujiang (January–December 1995) (%)

	Zhen jiang	*Jiu jiang*
Social Coordinating Fund	18.5	9.7
When individual account is exhausted and employee has to pay 5% of medical expenses	26.5	7.1
Individual account	20.0	60.0
Those who did not use individual account	35.0	23.2

Source: R.H. Cai (1997).

at an annual rate of 47–50 per cent (Yuen and Yan, 1997). In 1995 per capita expenditure under the government-funded health system represented about 18 per cent of an average worker's annual wage; similarly per capita expenditure in the labour insurance system for enterprises also represented some 18 per cent of the average wage (G.X. Cai, 1997). Thus a 10 per cent employer-contribution rate for the new health insurance scheme as in the two *jiangs* will definitely not be sufficient to cover the cost of rising medical bills unless some effective means can be found to drastically reduce hospital costs. It is reckoned that enterprises in Guangzhou are at present already devoting an equivalent of some 30 per cent of their wage bill to various types of social insurance, which puts an undue burden on their operating budget, bearing in mind that a lot of SOEs are in deficit. An important dilemma is how to pitch the contribution rate at a level which is both affordable by enterprises but realistic enough to meet the costs of healthcare.

The extent of coverage of the health insurance fund affects its financial viability. Current thinking in Guangzhou is to extend coverage on a phased basis, first to major illness, then to clinic treatment. At present the ratio between out-patient and in-patient consumption is about 70–75 : 30–25 per cent (G.X. Cai, 1997). If all out-patient services are to be borne by the individual account so that the social fund account will only be used to cater for major illnesses and hospitalization, then the pressure on individual savings will be significant which may create resentment on the part of employees, though this may help to curb patient demand. If the social fund portion in the overall insurance system is to be reduced to reflect the pattern of needs for out-patient versus in-patient services, then the social fund may become too small to perform the function of community risk pooling.

Failure to address provider problems

The new insurance scheme's three-tier financing arrangements should encourage the use of personal account savings and co-payment to meet employees' normal healthcare expenditure, which should both discourage unnecessary demand and also provide an affordable health financing system. This should help to alleviate problems on the demand side to some extent, and generate a reasonable financial basis to take care of the health needs of the urban working population, but it has not addressed the problem of rising costs on the supply side in hospitals despite the introduction of drug lists and treatment lists for the purpose of reimbursement.

Part of the supply-side hazard lies with the existing hospital management structure whereby hospitals are subjected to fragmented lines of control. There are at least three sorts of hospital in China, namely: (a) 'health' hospitals directly controlled by the central Ministry of Health and those sponsored by provincial, city and other local government health authorities; (b) 'military' hospitals sponsored by the Central Military Commission and district military authorities; and (c) 'occupational' hospitals run by institutions such as the Ministry of Railway and the Civil Aviation Administration. These various types of hospital do not subject themselves to any cost control regime which can be imposed by the specific local health insurance fund. Given the lack of sufficient state budget funds over the years, hospitals have all resorted to charging higher hospital fees and developed businesses on the side for the generation of revenue, notably the sale of drugs.[3] In Guangzhou, for example, it was reported that 25–35 per cent of hospital revenue came from non-medical sources, including drugs (Lee, 1997, p.34). As it stands, the proposed health insurance fund for the urban working population is 'hard' on the containment of patient demand and 'soft' on the containment of cost in hospitals.

Hospital grievances

The present healthcare reforms have only touched on the financing of health insurance but have largely ignored how to ensure that health providers are properly funded and whether there are sufficient mechanisms and processes to contain medical costs. Because hospitals are seriously underfunded, they tend to rely on high user fees and prescription charges in order to pay for staffing and operating costs. The government has also tried to allow some kind of *laissez-faire* environment so that hospitals can secure alternative income without seeking more government subsidy. This is not a satisfactory arrangement. As Lee's (1997, pp.34–5) field study in Guangzhou revealed, the hospital administrators were aggrieved by their 'sandwich position' during the reforms: on the one hand, the state endeavoured to economize and to cut its financial input into the medical system in the name of establishing a fiscal responsibility system; but on the other hand, the hospitals needed to make up the deficiency in state funding and to charge the patients additional fees, particularly for non-price-controlled services. Very often the government and the hospitals have been locked in constant friction over pricing policy and its enforcement (Lee, 1997, p.37).

Conflicting institutional interests and motives

It is suggested by some[4] that central or local 'health' authorities are not too enthusiastic about health finance reforms because they realize that such reforms might adversely affect hospital provider interests which they are supposed to safeguard as the latter's 'line' sponsors. For the central government, however, the main incentive in pushing for health insurance is to solve the problem of underfunding in government units and SOEs for employee healthcare. Part of the government's strategy to reform SOEs is to free them from the traditional socialist burden of providing for the full welfare of employees from cradle to grave. By allowing SOEs to lay off staff, to be relieved of the responsibility to provide housing, education and healthcare in kind, and even to go bankrupt, so as to give them a playing field level with that of private or foreign enterprises in the market, the government has to make sure that suitable protection schemes are available in society to cater for retirement pensions and unemployment payments to workers, as well as the provision of affordable 'privatized' housing, education and healthcare. So the government's overriding concern is to beef up enterprises' financial ability to support any such social security schemes introduced under SOE reforms. To the central government reformers, particularly those involved in economic system reform, health finance reform is merely an economic or funding question. They fail to recognize that in China's context of transiting from a previously centralized state-planning economy to a liberalized market economy, any changes are likely to bear significant administrative and social consequences. Health finance reform touches not only upon the interests of state finance, enterprise management and employees, but also upon those of state health personnel and their parent institutions, the hospitals.

Indeed, it is because of the lukewarm support from the Ministry of Health and its line bureaus and departments at the provincial/local levels that the State Council has had to involve the Ministries of Finance and Labour and the State Economic System Reform Commission in the pilot reform initiatives. However, in the process of introducing the two *jiang* experiment and extending it to other major cities, reformers concerned with the non-health aspects have tended to devote their efforts mainly to sorting out the sources of financing of the health insurance fund and the levels of contributions, overlooking the fact that hospital management reforms are of critical importance to any attempt to contain health expenditure. One way to curb provider costs is to turn hospitals into contracted service providers, (for example, on a pre-paid capitation basis) so that the funding agency, namely the health insurance fund, can have more leeway in negotiating with hospitals for more reasonable fees and more efficient services.

Community insurance coverage only for major illnesses

The intention behind most of the urban health insurance schemes is to induce workers to insure their own out-patient care and minor hospital charges through individual accounts and some form of co-payment, the social coordinating fund being used mainly to cover major illnesses and more expensive hospitalization. This is particularly the case in cities such as Beijing which have pursued an explicit *dabing tongcho* arrangement. As the World Bank (1997a, p.53) argued, while risk pooling which excluded catastrophic expenses did not make sense, there were on the contrary sound arguments for covering both catastrophic and some non-catastrophic expenses in a risk-pooling scheme because 'Insurance that covers only catastrophic care creates incentives to provide care in a hospital setting when less costly but often equally effective outpatient care might be available [and] it creates disincentives for consumers to seek early treatment,' which is typically more cost-effective.'

There are also problems with health insurance systems which put an emphasis on the utilization of savings accounts. In Singapore, where individual medical savings accounts are supplemented by public finance for the indigent and catastrophic insurance to cover any exceptionally high costs, per capita healthcare costs have actually grown by 13 per cent per year since 1984 when the Medisave system was introduced, 2 percentage points faster than before the change (World Bank, 1997a, p.65). Medical savings accounts tend to fail to realize the efficiency advantages of risk pooling because they give subscribers with good health an incentive to purchase healthcare even when it is unnecessary. While medical savings accounts and catastrophic insurance are most compatible with the type of fee-for-service payment methods now prevalent in Chinese cities, such a combination is also conducive to cost escalation and medically inappropriate care (World Bank, 1997a), not to mention the institutional inclination to overprescribe and overoperate that is already widespread in Chinese hospitals (as explained earlier).

Lack of momentum in rural health reforms

Drawing partly on lessons from the previous experience with the cooperative system (World Bank, 1997a, pp.51–2), a new policy for financing rural healthcare was announced in July 1994. The government called for the development of community-based schemes to fund and organize healthcare for the rural sector, guided by the following principles:

- each community organizes its own collective financing for basic healthcare
- funding will be drawn from multiple sources (government, collectives, and individuals)
- priority should be given to covering preventive services
- the schemes and benefit package should vary according to community conditions and economic capacity

Despite such exhortations, the situation remains that most provincial and county governments have found it difficult to set up voluntary community-financed schemes that require individual household contributions, given the already heavy tax burden on farmers. As the World Bank (1997a, p.52) suggested, 'China's villages and townships would have stronger incentives to develop community-based collective financing if the central government clarified and elaborated its priorities.' State subsidy is also necessary to shore up any rural community scheme's risk-pooling capacity.

Conclusion

To summarize, the major problems and limitations of China's health insurance reform process at this juncture are as follows.

1. The new insurance system comprising individual and community risk-pooling is confined to the cities and to urban workers, and has more or less the same coverage as previous government-funded healthcare and labour insurance healthcare.
2. The rural sector, made up of the bulk of the national population, is essentially neglected, despite some preliminary efforts to revive cooperative healthcare and community risk-pooling.

3. The claimed success of the two *jiang* experience cannot be easily extended to other municipalities due to demographic and cost structure reasons, so that the effective containment of escalating medical costs still poses the most challenging task to the various reform initiatives. In some places, such as Shenzhen and Beijing, there is an undue sharing of the cost burden by the individual workers in order to make the social coordinating fund financially viable, but such a lopsided arrangement is definitely not attractive to more lowly paid workers in the many economically less affluent cities.

4. All of the reform schemes implemented so far have failed to cover dependants of the workers. This may appear reasonable in terms of a contributory system, but it fails to address an important burden on the finances of government and enterprise units which are still obliged to take care of the dependants of their employees in some way. How to societalize the health insurance protection of these members of society remains unanswered.

5. The present stage of healthcare reform only deals with the financial problems. Others issues, notably the prescription and administration of drugs, and the management structure of health authorities and hospital institutions, must also be properly addressed before a cost-effective and socially affordable and equitable healthcare system can be set in place.

The new health insurance system based on the two *jiang* approach seeks mainly to find a substitute for the previous government-funded and labour insurance health systems in the urban areas, primarily to cater to the health protection needs of government and SOE workers. There is still the need to broaden the coverage to include the uninsured in the cities, such as dependants of employees and the growing proportion of the labour force that works outside the state sector. The inclusion of non-state workers may not be entirely easy, as the Shenzhen experience showed; there, joint ventures and private enterprises are reported to be reluctant to join in social health insurance (World Bank, 1997a, p.60). One possibility is to make participation of all enterprises and employment units in urban health insurance funds mandatory, so as to facilitate better urban risk-pooling. Another option is to leave it to the market, so that private voluntary insurance may eventually be encouraged to emerge to cater to the needs of non-state and thus uninsured employees, particularly those earning higher incomes and who are desirous of better health security.

Ultimately it is the vast rural population which warrants some urgent policy action. Urban health insurance reforms are only active on the government's policy agenda because of their implications for enterprise reforms and public finance reforms, where the objective is to make individual workers take over from government organs and state enterprises some of the financial responsibility for their welfare. But when this urban population – which accounts for only 10 per cent of the total population – is already taking up some two-thirds of medical costs (World Bank, 1997a, p.47), it is clear that developing appropriate communal or cooperative risk-pooling schemes in rural areas should instead be the most imperative task of the reformers. Unfortunately, as with its predecessors throughout history, the Chinese peasantry has tended to feature only marginally in successive national governments' policy considerations because political power still stays firmly in the cities.

In whatever way, a pure market model does not seem to be the answer to China's health problems. The introduction of health insurance funds in the cities does not represent a path of privatization in terms of surrendering state responsibilities to the market. For one thing, there is no active health market which can accept such a transfer of responsibilities without jeopardizing national health. A private insurance market to supply health insurance usually develops only in the most affluent urban populations (Musgrove, 1996), and does not guarantee equity in the access to basic care. Besides, any wholesale privatization will result in less control over health costs, which will cause widespread discontent in the urban working population. With the recent SOE reforms and government downsizing initiatives, state workers and cadres are also subject to serious anxiety over job and income security. Urban worker unrest and protests are now no longer a rarity. Politically, government leaders cannot afford to risk such discontent simply for the sake of privatization.

If one takes a maximalist approach to the notion of privatization, then any attempt on the part of the state to reduce the degree of its intervention, whether in terms of service provision, subsidy or regulation, could be regarded as a form of privatization (Le Grand and Robinson, 1984). However, in the case of China, what has been witnessed so far is not outright withdrawal of the state from social security, but a state-directed process of redefining the role of the state and reconfiguring the social support system by replacing direct state provision or state-financed enterprise/*danwei* provision with a society-based social insurance scheme, as in the case of health insurance reform. Such a trend represents a pendulum reversal from the previous 'big state, small society' (*da zhengfu, xiao shehui*) regime of the pre-reform era to a 'small state, big society' (*xiao zhengfu, da shehui*) environment which the Chinese reformers are ultimately trying to develop. As such, rather than privatizing healthcare, the present emphasis is on the shift from state control of social responsibilities to societalization of such responsibilities, with the 'societal' aspect still remaining prominent, even though in the process of change the responsibility of the individual is brought back in, in the form of individual contributions to the new insurance schemes.

In essence China's health insurance reforms seek to readjust the mix of state (community), enterprise and employee responsibilities within a reconfigured scheme. By including employees' contributions (though at a rather nominal level of 1 per cent of wage income) and maintaining their own individual account as the first port of call for resources to cover healthcare payments, there is certainly a new emphasis on the role and responsibility of the individual, which ties in well with the current ethos of economic reform. But given the community risk-pooling features of the new scheme, the process is more one of *societalization* (creating the new social funds to replace the state budget) than of *privatization per se*. Besides, health provider institutions and personnel remain largely state-owned/-employed and are subject to an administrative and budgeting regime of a different kind. Societalization is part of the larger project of the post-Mao Chinese Communist reformers to gradually but persistently dilute the previous statist features of employment benefits and social care. It was projected (Z.F. Liu, 1995, pp.34–5) that by the year 2000, for example, the burden of state and enterprises in the provision of such benefits and care would be reduced from 55 per cent in 1993 to 45 per cent of the expenditure. The share of responsibility of employees would increase from 8 per cent to 23 per cent, although 10 out of the 15 percentage points would be covered by transfer from the existing government/enterprise expenditure on relevant services to the wages of the employees.

The achievements made in the various pilot reform initiatives thus far have only managed to secure a generally workable form of societalization. Those in the urban areas who used to be insured are now given continued coverage, though requiring more individual co-payment responsibility, but the scope of coverage is still rather limited. The reforms have not yet moved forward to tackle the more difficult conditions of the vast rural population. They have also to be modified along the way to incorporate insurance protection for the growing non-state urban sector which lies outside the traditional protection net. All of these would represent still more challenges to the unenviable task of the health insurance reformers in China well into the twenty-first century. Premier Zhu Rongji's pledge to achieve health finance reform within three years (made in March 1998, after assuming the premiership) is probably too ambitious to be true, though it is fair to say that such reform is too important to the well being of the Chinese population to be delayed in any way.

Notes

1. Healthcare costs were generally established at 5.5 per cent of the enterprises' total wage expenditure.
2. During the heyday of the Cultural Revolution, the Red Guards, at the encouragement of Mao Zedong and the so-called 'revolutionaries', were determined to smash the 'urban old master Health Ministry' (*chengshi laoye weishengbu*).
3. Hospitals are allowed to retain 20 per cent of the price margin in the sale of drugs.
4. Interview with researchers of Guangzhou Academy of Social Sciences in May 1998.

5
Education Policy Reform

Ka-Ho Mok

In the post-Mao era, reformers have taken significant steps to privatize social policy and social welfare services. Since the adoption of a socialist market system in the 1990s, educational development has been affected by strong market forces. Despite the post-Mao leaders' discomfort with the term privatization, signs of state withdrawal from the provision of social welfare are clear. This chapter argues that the emergence of private educational institutions, the shift of state responsibility in educational provision to families and individuals and the prominence of fee-charging, as well as the introduction of internal competition among educational institutions, clearly suggest that China's education has been going through a process of marketization. Though the Chinese experience of marketization may be different from the West, there is no doubt that education is increasingly marketized. The principal goal of this chapter is to examine the institutional origins of the policy change in education, with particular reference to the process and implications of such changes. The chapter will also appraise the Chinese experience in the light of global practices regarding marketization of social policy.

Rationales, assumptions and features

The underlying assumption of adopting a market-oriented approach to restructuring education is that 'the empowerment of parents and students through resources-related choices in education has the potential to produce greater responsiveness and academic effectiveness' (Chubb and Moe, 1992, quoted in Grace, 1995, p.206). It is also assumed that private providers should be free to establish schools and to compete with each other, and thus people will have more choices in schooling.

Another rationale for employing market mechanisms is that customers themselves are the real and best judges about what they really want to buy in the education market.

In the process, several major features can be found: the clear private–public distinction between state activities and those of the market have become blurred; traditionally private sector practices are becoming more popular in the public sector; there is residualization of the universal provision of many state services; there are also changing practices of decentralization and devolution and an emphasis on market individualism. In his studies of educational reforms in the UK and elsewhere, Ball identified five major elements in the education market place: *choice, competition, diversity, funding* and *organization* (1990, p.61).

By *choice* we mean that parents should be provided with a choice of different types of schooling in terms of curriculum, language of instruction, education provision and school ethos. Advocates for market education believe *competition* between schools would best serve not only the consumers (parents and students), but also the nation by ensuring an orientation to 'continuous adaptation'. When school funding is directly linked to the performance of individual schools, it is argued that the introduction of 'internal competition' can ensure quality education. Another principle of the education market is closely related to the *diversity* of 'products' to make choice a real one for parents (consumers). More importantly, 'a real market is driven by rewards and by failure' (Ball, 1990, p.63). Following this logic, the choices made by the consumers should have a direct impact on *funding*, thereby rewarding those performing well but penalizing those less competitive ones by allocating fewer resources. The last aspect of the education market is to improve school management and initiate reforms/re-engineering in *organization*. Figure 5.1 shows these five major elements in marketizing education.

Central to the notion of marketization of education is 'a process whereby education becomes a commodity provided by competitive suppliers, educational services are priced and access to them depends on consumer calculations and ability to pay' (Yin and White, 1994, p.217). According to Buchbinder and Newson (1990), marketization takes two distinct forms: the first involves attempts by educational institutions to market their academic wares in the commercial world, while the other aims to restructure educational institutions in terms of business principles and practices. These two forms of marketization are also known as 'inside-out' and 'outside-in' practices to make the delivery of educational services more efficient and cost-effective. In short,

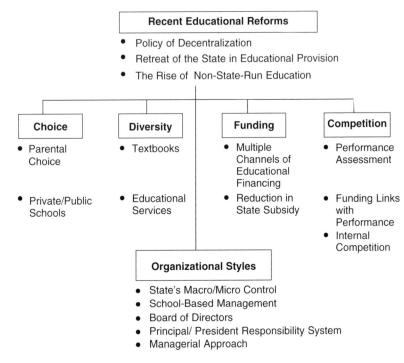

Figure 5.1 The education market place: recent educational restructuring in mainland china

Source: Modified from Ball (1990, p.60).

the adoption of a market-oriented approach in running education would have the following consequences:

- adoption of the fee-paying principle in education
- reduction in state provision, subsidy and regulation
- popularity of revenue-generating activities
- market-driven courses and curricula
- emphasis on parental choice
- managerial approach in educational administration/management

Having discussed some major conceptual issues related to education and the market place, the following sections will examine whether China's experience of marketization has been similar. If so, the implications of the marketization of China's education will be examined. Much of the material reported in the chapter is based on my field visits and intensive interviews conducted in the mainland over the last few years.

Economic growth and educational development

As the market economy develops, more and more people have internalized a new set of values, notably the acceptance of individual striving and market competition. Notions such as personal interest, material incentives, differential rewards, economic efficiency and market distribution are in the ascendant (Wong and Mok, 1996). Alongside this there is a rise in conspicuous consumption and an acceptance of consumerism (Hu *et al.*, 1989; Chai, 1992). Thus, as people have become more wealthy and are able to afford better education, self-financing and fee-charging principles have been initiated and implemented since the mid-1980s. Unlike the view prevailing in the Mao era that it was the state's sole responsibility to provide learning opportunities, many now adhere to a new idea of social responsibility. Different surveys regarding people's views towards 'fee-charging' in school education and in higher education repeatedly report that most of the respondents (averaging over 70 per cent) believe that they should bear the responsibility of paying for tuition (Z. Zhang, 1994; Bray, 1996; Jing, 1996). People's enhanced spending power and the fundamental value change as regards social responsibilities have undoubtedly created a very favourable environment for the rise of private educational institutions, as well as other kinds of educational provision in China.

Institutional origins of marketization of education

Under the reign of Mao, the CCP regarded education as a way to indoctrinate people with socialist ideals, and the state exerted a tight control over educational provision. After the CCP had consolidated its political power, a nationalization policy which included education was implemented. After 1956, all private schools were converted into public schools under the leadership of the Ministry of Education of the State Council (China National Institute of Educational Research, 1995). The adoption of a centralization policy in the educational sphere gave the central government relatively tight control over financing, provision and management of education. For decades, Chinese citizens had been accustomed to free education provided by the state (Yao, 1984).

The economic reforms have propelled China into a new stage of development. Economic modernization has not only fostered the growth of a market economy but has also caused a structural change in education. Under the slogan of 'socialist construction', the CCP has tried to reduce its involvement in the direct provision of educational services. In the immediate post-Mao era, the CCP initiated a decentralization policy in the educational realm to allow local governments, local communities, individuals and even other non-state actors to create more educational opportunities. Reshuffling the monopolistic role of the state in educational provision and reform in the educational structure started in the mid-1980s, and it has resulted in a mix of private and public consumption (Cheng, 1995a; Hayhoe, 1996; Mok, 1996). A policy paper entitled 'The Decision to Reform the Educational System' issued in 1985 by the Central Committee of the CCP indicated the state's resolve to 'diversify educational services by encouraging all democratic parties, people's bodies, social organizations, retired cadres and intellectuals, collective economic organizations and individuals subject to the Party and governmental policies, actively and voluntarily to contribute to developing education by various forms and methods' (Wei and Zhang, 1995, p.5).

In 1987, the 'Provisional Regulations on the Establishment of Schools by Societal Forces' gave further detail and more concrete legal guidelines on the establishment and management of non-state schools (Zhu, 1996). Coinciding with 'multiple channels' in financing, the state describes the use of a mixed economy of welfare as a 'multiple-channel' (*duoqudao*) and 'multi-method' (*duofangfa*) approach to the provision of educational services during the 'primary stage of socialism' (*shehui zhuyi chuji jieduan*), indicating a diffusion of responsibility from the state to society (Cheng, 1990; Mok, 1996).

Openly recognizing the fact that the state alone can never meet people's pressing educational needs, the CCP has deliberately devolved responsibilities to other non-state sectors to engage in educational development. In late 1993, 'The Programme for Reform and the Development of China's Education' stipulated that the national policy was to actively encourage and fully support social institutions and citizens attempting to establish schools according to laws, to provide appropriate guidelines and to strengthen administration (CCP Central Committee, 1993). Article 25 of the education law promulgated in 1995 reaffirmed once again that the state would give full support to enterprises, social institutions, local communities and individuals to establish schools under the legal framework of the People's Republic of China (State Education Commission, 1995). In short, the state's attitude towards the development of non-state-run education can be summarized by the phrase 'active encouragement, strong support, proper guidelines, and sound management' (*jiji guli, dali zhichi, zhengque yindao, jiaqiang guanli*). Under such a legal framework and in the context of the decentralization policy, China's education has been significantly affected by strong market forces. I would argue that such changes clearly suggest that education in China is going through a process of marketization. Let us now examine the major features of marketized education in mainland China.

Features of marketized education

Towards user charges

In line with the 1985 programmatic document 'Decision of the Central Committee of the Communist Party of China on the Reform of the Educational Structure' and 'The Outline of Education Reform and Development in China' promulgated by the Central Committee of the CCP and the State Council, local governments and educational practitioners have searched for 'multiple channels' for the financing of education (Cheng, 1990). Instead of relying upon the state's financial support, educational funding has been diversified by seeking other resources such as overseas donations, financial support levied from local government taxes and subsidies, and tuition fees (Mok, 1996).

Realizing that the state was financially unable to meet people's pressing need for educational services, the CCP adopted a policy of 'walking on two legs', whereby a shared responsibility between the state and the people was developed in financing primary education (Cheng, 1995a). In order to mobilize local communities, enterprises, individuals and even the market to engage in education, the state promoted a scheme of sponsorship at three levels: village, township and county. Under this scheme, the state would not bear more than one-third of the expenditure involved in the construction of school buildings and the purchasing of school furniture. What the state was responsible for was the payment of teachers' salaries. However, not all teachers are employed by the state. In the case of teachers working for *minban* (people-run) schools, their salaries are paid by their school authorities, who mainly derive funds from educational surcharges, local communities or tuition fees, as well as collecting taxes for educational use from local government. For most schools at village, township and county level, educational funding is generated mainly from the local community, tuition fees and overseas donations (Cheng, 1995b).

In the 1990s, the CCP further shifted the responsibility away from the state and towards individuals and families by the introduction of a fee-paying principle. Early in the 1980s, the plan for charging students fees was regarded as 'ultra-plan', implying that the intake of these 'self-supporting' students was beyond the state plan (Cheng, 1996). After the endorsement of a socialist market economy in the Fourteenth Party Congress, the State Education Commission (SEC) officially gave approval for institutions of higher education to admit up to 25 per cent of students in the 'commissioned training' or 'fee-paying' categories in 1992. In 1993, 30 higher learning institutions were selected for a pilot study for a scheme known as 'merging the rails', whereby students were admitted either because of public examination scores or because they were willing and able to pay a fee, although their scores were lower than the level normally required. In 1994, more institutions entered the scheme and the fee-charging principle was thus legitimized (Cheng, 1996). In this policy context, it is not surprising that in the past few years commissioned (*daipei*), self-supporting and quasi-private television university and correspondence university students have taken a bigger share of the total student population in China (Pepper, 1995; Hayhoe, 1996; Yuan and Wakabayashi, 1996).[1]

The structural change in the financing of education in China is more obvious in higher education. Before the 1990s, fee-paying students were only a very tiny group, but their numbers have been increasing since the adoption of the user charge principle. The percentage of fee-paying students at higher educational institutions in Shanghai grew from 7.5 per cent in 1988 to 32.1 per cent in 1994 (Yuan and Wakabayashi, 1996). Table 5.1 shows that the number of self-supporting students has expanded throughout the country since 1988.

In the higher education sector, Zhongshan University in Guangzhou, for instance, started to 'merge the tracks' in 1995, implying that there are no longer any differences between publicly-funded students, self-funding students and 'commissioned' students. This new trend is confirmed by prominent academics interviewed by the author. For instance, Professor Cai He, Head of the Department of Sociology, and Professor Zhang Minqiang, Director of the Institute of Higher Education of Zhongshan University, observed[2] that students had begun to accept the fee-paying principle. In the year 1997–98, the range of tuition fees varied across courses; students had to pay from 2500 to 3500 yuan (while the average per capita monthly salary in Guangzhou was around 1000 yuan in 1997). Wu Yechun, Deputy Director of the Office of Administration, South China University of Technology, also

Table 5.1 Enrolment changes in higher educational institutions in China, 1988–94

Year	Total number of students	Number of self-supporting students	%
1988	669 700	42 200	6.3
1989	579 100	25 800	4.5
1990	608 600	17 300	2.8
1991	616 000	11 800	1.9
1992	628 400	11 300	1.8
1993	924 000	336 000	36.4
1994	899 800	364 000	40.5

Source: Yuan and Wakabayashi (1996), p.195.

suggested that students had far more incentive to study hard after the adoption of a fee-charging principle in universities:

> In the past, university education was entirely supported by the state and students seemed to take higher education for granted and thus their motivation was low once they were admitted. But the situation has changed since the adoption of 'self-paying' principle in the university sector. Students are strongly motivated to study because they have to pay for the courses and they are eager to learn a wider range of subjects to broaden their knowledge base. Despite the fact that some students (particularly those who are from poor families) may have difficulties in paying for tuition fees, many of them are able to secure financial support to obtain higher education... More fundamentally, people are generally supportive of the 'fee-paying' principle in higher education because they believe that higher education is an investment. With higher qualifications university graduates would find it easier to get jobs in the open labour market; 'value' is thus added to the students after university training.
>
> (field interview, Guangzhou, March 1998)

Fee-charging is not unique to higher education; it has also been implemented in primary, secondary and vocational schools. Even though the official policy is to grant free education for Chinese citizens up to junior high school, miscellaneous charges are permitted (Cheng, 1995b, 1996; A. West, 1995; Bray, 1996). In Guangdong, a laboratory for the economic reforms and the most prosperous province in China, all students (from primary to tertiary level) pay for their tuition fees. Table 5.2 shows that, in 1993, students in senior high schools had to pay 2.5 times as much as students in junior high schools. Students are charged different fees according to where they live (West, 1995a). In order to generate sufficient funds for educational development, educationalists and school principals in Guangdong have tried to experiment with an 'Educational Reserves' model. The main characteristics of this model are: parents have to pay their children's tuition and miscellaneous fees in advance (for several years ahead), and this money forms educational reserves for developing educational facilities and services (*Jiaoyu Daokan*, 1, 1996, pp.7–10). Developments such as these are indicative of explorations of multiple channels of financing to support educational development.

The emergence of private education

The Fourteenth Congress of the CCP (1992) endorsed the principle of introducing the socialist market economy, thereby creating a favourable environment for the emergence of private education (Mok, 1996). To foster further economic development in China, the State Education Commission issued the document 'Points Regarding How to Expedite Reforms and Vigorously Develop Ordinary Higher Education', giving key guidelines for how Chinese higher education might adapt itself to the socialist market economy (Yin and White, 1994). The development of private education was supported by the 'Provisional Regulations for the Establishment of People-Run Schools of Higher Education' promulgated in 1993 by the State Education Commission. In late 1993, 'The Programme for Reform and the Development of China's Education' stipulated that the national policy was actively to encourage and fully

Table 5.2   China: average miscellaneous fees and unit costs (yuan per student per year), 1993

Type of school	Tuition and other fees	Total unit cost	Fee as a share of unit cost (%)
General senior high	118	917	12.9
General junior high	47	477	9.9
Rural general junior high	44	413	10.7
Primary	23	247	9.3
Rural primary	22	225	9.8
Rural vocational	182	993	18.3

Source: A. West 1995, cited in Bray (1996), p.18.

support social institutions and citizens to establish schools according to laws and to provide the right guidelines and strengthen administration (CCP Central Committee, 1993).

Under such a legal framework, different types of school systems have thrived. Privately-run educational institutions have also become popular in the big cities (Mok and Chan, 1996). Realizing the importance of education, Chinese citizens believe that having higher education may enable them to earn more money. Many surveys report that people view education as vital to career development. A survey in Shanghai found that more than 60 per cent of parents want their children to receive higher education (Z. Zhang, 1996). Another survey carried out by the Central Education Science Institute in Guangzhou in 1993 showed that 73 per cent of the 500 respondents favoured the establishment of non-governmental schools at the basic education level (Z. Zhang, 1996). Under this favourable policy environment, non-state run educational institutions ranging from kindergartens to higher learning institutions have developed rapidly.

By 1994, there were more than 800 non-state higher educational institutions across the nation, of which 18 were fully recognized by the State Education Commission with authority to grant their own diplomas (China National Institute of Educational Research, 1995, p.11). According to Xiang and Gu (1996), by the end of 1993 there were 60 000 non-state run schools and colleges (including schools run by the private sector) on the mainland, including 16 990 kindergartens, 4030 primary schools, 851 secondary schools and more than 800 tertiary institutes. A 1996 report suggested that the number of private/ *minban* institutions included around 20 780 kindergartens, 3159 primary/secondary schools, 672 secondary vocational schools and 1230 higher educational institutions (Cheng, 1997).

In 1998, there were three non-governmental higher education institutions in the Guangdong area and they have adopted different strategies to run their colleges. Hualian Private College, the first privately-owned higher education institution in Guangdong, primarily relies upon students' tuition fees for running costs; while the non-governmental [*Minban*] Nanhua Industrial and Business College is financed partially by students' tuition fees and partly supported by the Trade Union of Guangdong Province. Another newly established private college, Pei Zheng Business College, has adopted a *minban gongzhu* model (that is, people-run but publicly assisted). The college is financially supported by the local government (Hua Du City) in the form of a subsidized land premium to pay for the college building and teachers' salaries. In addition to local government support, Pei Zheng Alumni also raise funds for their *alma mater* (Wu, 1996; Mok, 1997a).

Realizing the pressing demand for higher education, these non-governmental institutions take advantage of the relatively liberal socio-political environment to develop courses and programmes catering for market needs. For instance, the Nanhua Industrial and Business College offers programmes falling into four major areas: law, catering and tourism, business management, and administrative management. In order to be competitive in the 'education market', the College has adopted a 'Five Gears Strategy'. First, courses are geared to the market. Second, courses are geared to availability. Third, English courses are geared to international needs. Fourth, education is geared to students' needs. And finally, the College is geared to becoming a famous school to attract more students (Niu, 1997). Professor Niu Xianmin, President of the College, acknowledged that students were the 'life-blood' of the College and the market had actually guided the development of non-governmental colleges (field interview, July 1995; Mok, 1997a).

Knowing that non-governmental higher education institutions would face immense difficulties in competing with the state-supported system, private colleges have a clear vision to differentiate themselves from formal higher education institutions by specializing in courses which are geared to newly emerging market needs. In addition, they are committed to serving the local communities wherever they are located. For example, Pei Zheng Business College has a mission to produce educated people for Hua Du City and has established a very close link with local enterprises to create more opportunities for its students through internship and placement experiences (Wu, 1996). Following a similar path, other non-governmental colleges are in the process of establishing themselves; the private Chaoshan College and Nanling College in Guangdong have already secured financial support from local government and are ready to begin operations in the near future (Wu, 1996).

More interestingly, private/*minban* education is also popular in Shanghai where a *minban gongzhu* approach has been adopted to create more educational opportunities. I visited several colleges of this kind in 1997 and 1998. Guang Qi College, one of these *minban gongzhu* colleges in Shanghai, was established in 1996 by Professor Chen Quanfu, Dean of Adult Education of Shanghai Jiao Tong University. When asked about the nature of *minban gongzhu*, Professor Chen said:

> *Minban gongzhu* means that the college is not entirely funded by the non-state sector but is partially supported by the government in

terms of financial support of school building. Guang Qi College is one of these *minban gongzhu* colleges. The Xuhui Qu, a local government in Shanghai, is committed to establishing a local higher educational institution to train educated people to assist in modernization and to match the needs of the local community created by rapid economic development. Therefore, the local government has given financial support to found the Guang Qi College in the hope of creating more people with knowledge and skills to serve in the local community.

(field interview, April 1998)

With support from local government in providing school buildings and financial aid, Guang Qi College was founded in October 1996 as a *minban gongzhu* college to serve local needs. Seeing a huge gulf between demand and supply in formal higher education, a group of old and experienced professors from Shanghai Jiaotong University and Fudan University therefore secured local government support to run a *minban* college. Calling itself a 'community-based' higher educational institution, Guang Qi has identified several selected areas for teaching, offering programmes which place an emphasis on practical knowledge, computing skills, foreign languages and advanced technology. Sharing the facilities and libraries of Shanghai Jiao Tong University, coupled with a stable teaching team comprised of retired but experienced professors from Fudan and Jiaoda, Guang Qi's success is reflected in its students' performance in public examinations. Its good record attracted 9000 applicants for only 250 places in the 1997/98 academic year.

The formation of Hua Xia College, another *minban gongzhu* college in Shanghai, was initiated by East China Normal University to create more learning opportunities for Shanghai citizens. Like Guang Qi College, Hua Xia College is another community-based college. Despite the fact that Hua Xia has not received formal recognition from the central government, it has been approved by the Shanghai municipal government and its foundation has received support from the local community and East China Normal University. With financial resources generated from tuition fees, overseas donations and the local community, Hua Xia was founded in August 1996. Enjoying a strong affiliation with East China Normal University, Hua Xia students can use its library and laboratory facilities. Additionally, Hua Xia has a degree of autonomy which its formal counterparts do not.

Realizing that the state alone can never meet the pressing demand for higher education, Professor Qian, President of Hua Xia College, is a firm advocate of *minban* colleges. These institutions have a useful role in filling the gap between the existing supply and demand in the formal university sector. Hence the central government should allow more autonomy to local educationalists and intellectuals to run *minban* colleges. It is also important that the state formally recognizes their teaching standards and qualifications. The case for *minban* colleges is aptly summarized by Professor Qian as follows:

> There is no harm at all in having *minban* colleges in China. First, we can create additional learning opportunities for students. Second, we can make use of the expertise, knowledge and experience of retired professors and they are very keen to serve and teach in the higher educational sector. Third, it is a better utilization of existing facilities and space than formal public universities. Calculating all these advantages together, I think the state must support and recognize the development of *minban* colleges.
>
> (field interview, May 1997)

Despite the fact that the state has not formally granted *minban* colleges university status, it has gradually accepted the existence of *minban* as a reality which it cannot deny. In the Education Law promulgated in 1995 and the most recent higher education law issued in 1998, the role of *minban* education has been formally recognized and proper systems and mechanisms will be worked out to monitor the qualifications awarded by, and the academic standards of, these colleges. No matter how the state perceives the role of *minban* higher educational institutions, there is no doubt that *minban* education has developed as a part of the educational system in the mainland. The discussion above has only focused on two major models of private/*minban* education. There are other approaches and models of non-state-run schools throughout the country.

Private/*minban* education is popular not only at the tertiary level but also in primary and secondary education. Zhonghua Yinghao School and Bigui Yuan School in Guangdong are two outstanding examples of this kind. School administrators and principals in these private schools consciously identify newly emerging market needs and design courses to fill the gap. To attract more students, these institutions stress their connections with schools and universities from other countries. By emphasizing the opportunities their students have for overseas exchange programmes, these schools can enhance their reputations (Mok and Chan, 1996; Kwong, 1997).

Private schools are often criticized for charging high tuition fees. Often they ask for large sums of money as debentures from the parents or set high tuition fees for courses. Notwithstanding these complaints, they are welcomed by many parents who believe it is a better choice for their children. Operating from a relatively prosperous financial position, these schools have more resources with which to manage and administer their programmes. Eschewing their dependence upon the state's financial support, non-state-run schools can be autonomous in areas such as academic and administrative structure, the design of curriculum, the hiring of academic and administrative staff, using 'flexible class duration' for various activities, as well as a lower staff–student ratio, and other academic-related activities (Mok and Chan, 1996; Mok, 1997a).[3]

All these developments suggest that educational services have become diversified; types of schools have emerged which are not state-run educational institutions and that has happened in response to market generated demands.

Competition among educational institutions

Drawing comparative insights from leading universities in other countries, the CCP has begun to realize the importance of bringing about substantial improvements in its university education. In order to enhance quality education at the tertiary level, the CCP introduced 'Project 211'. The idea is to attach new financial and strategic importance to about 100 universities and some subject areas in order to help these institutions become world-class universities early in the twenty-first century. Central to the scheme is a plan to introduce competition among universities and to reward the top 100 higher educational institutions. Universities are assessed by quantifiable objective criteria such as staffing, buildings, libraries, laboratories, research, funding and so on to determine whether they are qualified to be among the top. Once selected, the universities will attract more funding from the central government. To enhance their chances, many universities have tried to form mergers to improve their research and academic profile (Christiansen, 1996; Rosen, 1997). For instance, the old Shanghai University announced a plan to merge with other local colleges to become a more comprehensive university. After the merger the new Shanghai University proved itself a more competitive university and has been selected as one of the '211' universities. More significantly, the '211' programme means that 'internal competition' has been introduced among universities. Seemingly an internal market is evolving in China's university sector.

Following the introduction of competition in higher education, the resources and funds of individual universities are determined by their research output and the proportion of graduates getting employment. According to Hayhoe (1996), university authorities have a general expectation that staff in research institutions should spend two-thirds of their time on research and one-third on teaching, while the reverse expectation is commonly held in teaching institutions. Inevitably, when competition is introduced among higher educational institutions rewarding winners and showing up losers, faculty members have experienced intensified work pressure to improve their research profile.

In 1997, the SEC issued a new directive for higher education in the mainland. Universities are now being encouraged to share resources and facilities. There will be moves to merge universities to enhance research and teaching quality, to consolidate and strengthen existing good work, and to establish new universities in collaboration with local governments (Wu, 1997). Under such a policy directive, local universities in Guangzhou (the provincial capital of Guangdong) have attempted to merge with others to enhance their common strengths in the hope that they may be selected into the top 100. For instance, Guangzhou Normal University, Guangzhou Institute of Education and Guangzhou Teacher College will merge and form a new Guangzhou Normal University. At the same time, Guangzhou Medical College, South China Construction College and Guangzhou University are committed to improving their research and teaching, and to establishing closer links with local industries and businesses to make their courses more attractive and competitive in the market (Wu, 1997).

Another growth area will be the establishment of a 'University City' in Guangzhou. Realizing the limitations faced by the Guangzhou city-run higher education institutions, particularly in terms of the small size of the student population, limited space for school buildings and inadequate resources and faculty members, it is proposed that a University City could be developed, comprising various local institutions of higher learning such as Jiaotong College, the Vocational College, the Industrial and Business College, the College of Arts and Law, and the College of Finance. The proposed merger will draw resources and strengths together. Coupled with the existing 100 college-run research centres and enterprises, students are expected to benefit from sharing more resources, better facilities, well-qualified faculty members and enhanced research and teaching in the future University City (Wu, 1997).

Consumer choice

Considering students' choice as a very prominent factor affecting course design, educational institutions in China have adopted a customer-oriented approach to running their educational services. For instance, the Department of Teaching, People's University of China (Renda), conducted a survey on teaching matters among faculty members and concluded that new teaching materials must be introduced to cater for newly emerging market needs. Thereafter, a 'Textbook Revolution' was initiated by using and publicizing 100 new textbooks throughout the university in 1993. New teaching materials were written and compiled, and a special Teaching Material Working Committee was set up to coordinate comprehensive reform in teaching (Wei, 1996). In addition to teaching material reform, another major action which Renda has taken is to reshuffle the disciplines and specializations to cater for newly emerging needs from the market. Not unexpectedly, programmes such as international commerce, international enterprise management, marketing, taxation, national economic management, real estate business and management and so on have been introduced, and have successfully attracted many students.

One striking example is that of the Department of History at Zhongshan University, one of the key universities in China. The department has faced a drop in student numbers under the market economy. In order to attract more students, the department has started to re-package courses to make them more marketable. Courses such as 'culture and history' and 'tourism and history' have therefore been introduced, with similar practices also adopted by departments of pure academic studies. Applied value, such as courses in applied mathematics, applied physics and applied chemistry, has been emphasized to attract students. Similar cases can easily be observed elsewhere in China's schools, especially when one sees how often computer literacy, spoken English, diversified subjects and practical value are stressed in course design and curriculum development.

In order to please consumers, quality control systems and measures have been introduced. For instance, Hading Chemical Industry Institute proposed a reform measure called 'teachers hanging up their shingles and students choosing their own courses'. This means that, for the same course, classes with different specializations, requiring different amounts of study time, providing different amounts of credits, and using a diversity of teaching methods are employed. These are taught by teachers with varied teaching styles, each of whom 'hangs out' his or her 'shingle', and students may choose whichever teacher they like best. As a result, students face fierce competition if they wish to be personally taught by the best teachers. Teachers 'hanging out their shingles' is something new in Shanghai as well as throughout China.

Since the implementation of the system of teaching by 'shingle-hanging', teachers have acquired control over students' examinations and grading, and students have a degree of influence on control of teachers' teaching standards and the amount of wages and bonuses teachers receive. More importantly, the scheme is seen as a means to raise teachers' sense of responsibility towards teaching. In addition, this reform is used to inspire excellence and to encourage everyone to put all their energies into teaching and research. This institute also introduces competition among faculty, rewarding those working hard with monetary prizes to induce faculty members to engage actively in research activities (Wei, 1996, pp.84–8). Educational services are priced, and access to them depends on consumer calculations and the ability to pay. All in all, the re-focusing of curricula towards a more practical orientation and emphasizing the importance of vocational training and responsiveness to student and market demand are significant indications that China's education has been going through a marketization process (Yin and White, 1994; Mok, 1997a).

Revenue generation

Unlike the Mao era when educational development was entirely directed by the central government, there has been a strong tide of diversification and decentralization of education in post-reform China. Starting from the mid-1980s onwards, senior leaders of the CCP have begun to encourage administrators, principals and presidents of schools and universities to search for additional funding to run educational services (Mok and Wat, 1998). In 1988, Zhao Ziyang, the former Party Secretary, openly admitted that the state did not have sufficient funds to meet the pressing demands for education. He therefore encouraged educational institutions to join in the nationwide proliferation of commercial activities. Similarly, Li Peng, the former commissioner of education in 1987, also urged local governments to multiply financial sources to support educational development. It is in such a policy context that *chuang shou* (income-generating activity) was initiated and officially endorsed (Kwong, 1996).

In order to generate more income to support educational development, school principals and university administrators have ventured into the business and commercial fields to get extra funding. Through the opening of business firms and enterprises (*xiaoban qiye*), running commissioned courses, offering adult education and evening courses to attract more students, or charging consultant fees are becoming more popular. Other means include schools renting out premises, running cafeterias, salons, bars or even turning assembly halls into discos or places for entertainment (Kwong, 1996; Mok, 1997a, 1998).

Many of the renowned universities in the mainland now run business firms to create additional educational funds. Peking University (Beida) is one of these higher educational institutions which engages in business and commerce to obtain extra funds to support teaching and research. A new mode of education – 'integrate the school and business units, support the schools with factories' – has gained momentum among many schools and colleges. Ren Yanshen, Vice-Secretary of the Party Committee of Beida, believes that the universities' ventures into commerce and business could support their scholastic and research work. The income thus obtained can be used to improve teaching conditions, provide teachers and staff with opportunities to exercise their professional skills, and relieve them of anxieties about their livelihood (Ren, cited in Wei, 1996, pp.72–3). Qinghua University, another key university distinguished by its leadership in science and technology, has run factories and business firms for years. In addition, many in its faculty have established close links with the industrial sector, playing either the role of consultant or a managerial role in some enterprises (Pepper, 1995; N. Zhou, 1995; Mok, 1998).

According to another report, among 50 higher educational institutions, there are 238 companies, 144 factories and 43 joint ventures (*sanzi qiye*), diverting about 40 per cent of company profits to support scholastic activities (N. Zhou *et al.*, 1996). Other methods, such as 'holding international conferences and charging registration fees to foreign participants, conducting training courses for local industry workers, organizing tours to Chinese archaeological sites, assisting in computerization activities [for] businesses, offering preparatory courses for individuals who may wish to pursue advanced degrees and so on are also organized (Julius, 1997, p.148). With additional income gained from venturing into the 'commercial sea', educational institutions can allocate more money to raise the salaries of teachers and improve teaching and research facilities (*China News Analysis*, 15 October, 1993; Cheng, 1996).

Consequences

Disparity in educational development

By allowing multiple channels of financing education, particularly from the non-governmental sectors, the CCP has witnessed the spread of regional disparities due to the uneven development of various regions in the country, with poorer western provinces lagging far behind the richer southern and eastern provinces in terms of educational development. This is happening not only in public schools and universities, but in private schools and tertiary institutions as well (Cheng, 1997).

The decentralization of finance for schooling puts regional disparity into sharper focus as poorer communities lack the funds to ensure quality education in their schools. In this way schools and tertiary institutions are trying to grasp the meaning of educational reform, while engaging in fund-raising endeavours of various types as well as other kinds of activity that may help them to find their own place in the newly changing educational system (Mok and Chan, 1998). Even within the more fully developed coastal province of Guangdong, there is also disparity between the cities and the rural areas. As discussed earlier, in Guangdong, some parents can afford to pay 300 000 yuan as a debenture for getting their children a place in Private Yinghao School (Mok and Chan, 1996), while people living in Liannan, a poor rural county, have limited educational opportunities and suffer from poor school facilities (*Po Yin Newsletter*, October 1997). Disparity is found not only in urban and rural parts of Guangdong but also within Guangzhou city. A study in Guangzhou reveals that disparities in educational provisions between the city centre and the city outskirts are evident (Lee and Li, 1994). If disparity is easily found in Guangzhou, one of China's most prosperous cities, it is not too difficult to imagine its spread in other parts of the country.

As a whole, it is fair to say that disparities exist between regions in terms of educational opportunities, resources and schools facilities, teacher qualifications and student attainments. Factors leading to these differences vary, and are probably a combination of historical factors and regional developmental processes, as well as governmental policies relating to remuneration for teachers in the central city and teachers in the counties. In addition, rapid economic development in the city may well lead to educational disparities based on families' socio-economic backgrounds (Davis, 1995; Pepper, 1995).

Equality and quality

Education can help people to improve their potential to manage their resources and improve their health. At the same time, economic development and the educational level of the population are interdependent. Despite the fact that more people in mainland China have enjoyed better educational opportunities in the past decades, many in the rural areas have not benefited from formal education. According to a study of the quality of education and academic performance of students, the academic performance of students in the eastern and middle regions is better than that in the western provinces. The same study also reveals that there is a close relationship between economic development, educational development and quality of education (Xie *et al.*, 1997, p.14). Comparing the average scores and pass rates of all subjects among the three regions, both primary pupils and secondary students in the eastern and middle regions have better results than students in the western part of China (Xie *et al.*, 1997).

When education is marketized, the new financial structure has unquestionably allowed the richer areas to do more with their abundant resources. Meanwhile, the poorer places are left behind as a result of their limited means to develop education. Thus, if the principal of a school can bring in more resources, it will mean more and better facilities for the school. It will also mean that the school can attract more qualified teachers and better students. The result is an improvement in the quality and quantity of education, as well as in its form and substance. But what is also true is that financial resources are inadequate for those poorer regions, and hence educational opportunities are not equally distributed to Chinese citizens. The marketization of education does raise the issue of equality of education.

In addition, marketization of education has also led to varied academic performance among different regions which, in turn, shapes their educational development. With more resources allocated to education, big cities on the coast offer far better opportunities. With an abundant supply of qualified and well-educated people, the eastern seaboard has an enhanced ability to further develop its economy. In contrast, people in the interior suffer from limited opportunities, which inevitably weakens their position to compete with the coastal regions in the open market.

Ownership

With school management and finance devolved to the local level, the issue of ownership has become very controversial as the central government still wants to uphold its final decision-making power when it comes to the final say about what can or cannot be done. In the past few years, while carrying out research on private and *minban* education in the mainland, I have observed that once the policy of decentralization was adopted in the 1980s, it became extremely difficult for the state to impose or maintain control. Capitalizing on the relatively liberal and favourable policy environment, local leaders and experts in the educational field have exercised more freedom and autonomy in terms of school administration and management, the design of the curriculum, and control over staffing and financial matters (Mok, 1997b). My most recent study of education in Guangdong and Shanghai again shows that educationalists and academics there are very much aware of the importance of autonomy and freedom in educational development. Many of the interviewees said that they would be very happy to extend their control over the educational sphere by eschewing dependence on state grants. Adopting different strategies to generate additional revenue, educational institutions have been able to have more say in the development plans of their institutions, especially when they become more financially independent. Some interviewees believe that the state should accept and support private education. They argue that while the private element has been well recognized and accepted in the economic realm, the state should also allow the private sector to develop in the educational sphere in the socialist market environment. Many interviewees even support private ownership in education, especially when an education market has already emerged. All in all, the diversification of educational services and the emergence of non-state-run educational institutions have raised the issue of educational ownership. This issue is an important one and needs to be addressed properly by the government.

Conclusion

In the light of the conceptual framework at the beginning of the chapter, namely the adoption of a fee-charging principle, the diversification of educational services offered by the non-state sector, the creation of market-driven courses and curricula, the introduction of internal competition in the educational sector and revenue-generation activities, it is evident that education in China has been going through a process of marketization. Even though the state has not deliberately set out to promote private education, the state's persistent call for decentralization and diversification of educational services has created ample room for the growth of private education, and has also created a much more mixed economy within the public sector. Even though the state has never called for the development of an education market in the mainland, it is beyond doubt that the recent educational restructuring in China shows all the major elements of a movement towards an education market. As a consequence of the process of marketization, diversity of services and consumers' choice have received due attention, internal competition is introduced to ensure quality education, funding is determined by performance and a managerial approach is adopted in the quality assurance process. Putting all the observations discussed above together, it can be argued that the recent transformation of China's educational realm has taken two forms of marketization, as Buchbinder and Newson suggested (1990): both 'inside-out' and 'outside-in' approaches have been adopted in an attempt to make the delivery of educational services more efficient and responsive to market needs.

Despite the process of marketization, true internal markets in Chinese education have not yet evolved. The split between purchaser and provider is not clear in China's educational realm (Mok, 1997a). The strategies adopted by the CCP to create more educational opportunities in response to emerging market needs are highly instrumental. The aim is to improve administrative efficiency and effectiveness as well as resolve the fiscal crisis which the state is now encountering, rather than to make a fundamental shift of value orientation. This is because the CCP has never committed itself theoretically and ideologically to public choice theory or economic rationalism, the philosophical basis of marketization and privatization. It is worth noting that even though China's education has been going through a process of marketization, the CCP still fears that the emergence of private education in the mainland will greatly challenge the conventional order. In spite of the fact that the traditional social/public policy paradigm practised in the Mao era has proved to be ineffective in the socialist market context (Wong, 1998), the state still has a problem with openly acknowledging the ideological conflict between socialism and the principles of market economy. This point is clearly revealed by the condemnation of the private element in the educational sector by banning profit-making institutions (Mok and Chan, 1996). Trying to uphold the socialist ideal so that the legitimacy of the CCP can be maintained, the CCP has tried very hard to protect this last 'battle-field' of socialism: public education.

However, the CCP's efforts to protect the last 'bastion' of a planned economy may prove to be ineffective, especially when the public and state-run schools are starting to look private. The discussion above has already demonstrated how schools and universities in the public sector have begun by choice and necessity to adopt market principles and strategies in refashioning their courses. A fee-charging system is not only operating in non-state-run schools, but state-run and even key-point schools are also using similar strategies in financing education. Public schools are very active in business activities to raise revenue (N. Zhou *et al.*, 1996). There has been a strong trend in China's educational realm towards diversity and plurality because the state has deliberately de-monopolized its role as service provider. Local initiatives, individual efforts and the private sector have all tried to create more educational opportunities, resulting in a division of labour between the state, local government, the community, and the school. As a result, diversity and variety can now be found not only in the structure of education but also in the design of curricula and textbooks (Cheng, 1995a; Mok, 1997c). Particularly striking is the phenomenon that publicly-run educational institutions are becoming more marketized.

The Chinese experience of marketization of education suggests that the private and public boundary is blurring. In this regard, the most crucial question in the debate over the public and private distinction is not to do with being public or private: in order to reduce the burden of the state in educational provision, economic factors are considered by public administrators to be the most important ones, and it is economic considerations that drive individuals and shape social and public policy. The university sector is not the only sector affected by strong market forces: other fields (such as welfare, health, and housing) are going through a similar trend of marketization. Reductions in state subsidy, provision and regulation, and a transfer of state responsibility to other non-state sectors are good indicators of the breakdown of public/private borders. The growing impact of market forces on the educational realm has inevitably led to a border-crossing process, whereby both public and private schools in the mainland have to make themselves more competitive in a market environment. In this regard, a discussion of educational marketization would seem to include not only schools that call themselves private but also public schools that in many ways appear increasingly to be private, thus making the distinction between private and public more problematic.

In addition, the retreat of the state has also led to a process of renegotiation between the state and society of their division of social responsibilities, and eventually to a new definition of the state/society relationship in general and public/private boundaries in particular

(Mok, 1997b,c). Thus the public/private debate is essentially related to the question of '*how* [people] choose between public and private provision and *how* [they] establish the proper balance between them' (Wilding, 1990, p.27). What is clear, then, is that the future of educational provision in China lies in a much more overtly mixed economy.

Notes

1. From the mid-1980s onwards, the CCP decided to secure selective recovery of higher educational costs. In addition to charging tuition fees, the government restructured its financial support system for students by introducing loans for those who cannot afford to pay for higher costs in education (see, for example, Li and Bray, 1992).
2. Interview.
3. The discussion here refers only to these private/*minban* schools with good financial backing such that they can initiate new methods and adopt innovative approaches to education. None the less, this might not be true for those *minban*/private schools without adequate educational funds.

6
Housing Reform

K.Y. Lau and James Lee

Housing reform in China constitutes a major part of a wider economic reform. Over the last 15 years, major cities such as Shanghai, Beijing, Guangzhou and Shenzhen have experimented with various reform packages, with the common goal of transferring the ownership of bulk state housing properties now in the hands of state-owned enterprises or housing bureaus to individual consumers. These housing experiments met with varying degrees of success, with some achieving a higher degree of marketization than others. The focus of housing reform is to recapitalize public sector housing and make the housing supply available through the market.

Housing reform in China has never emerged as a blueprint from the planning table. More aptly put, it is a pragmatic and incremental response to the aftermath of the Cultural Revolution, which brought China's economic development almost to a standstill. While major cities such as Beijing and Shanghai received substantial housing investment in the form of new public housing in the first 15 years after the Communist take-over in 1949, the subsequent political turmoil has devastated nearly all major housing projects. When millions of urban youths returned to major cities from the countryside after the Cultural Revolution ended in 1976, housing became an acute urban problem. To tackle the housing shortage, Deng described his broad directives regarding housing reform in 1980 as follows:

> Urban residents should [be allowed to] buy their own houses, or to build their own houses. Not just new houses could be sold, old houses could as well. Payment could be made in lumpsum or by instalments of 10 to 15 years' length. Public sector rentals must be adjusted. Otherwise no one will buy. Different rents should be

charged for different locations. When rents have been increased, extra rent subsidies should be given to low wage earners. New houses could be jointly developed between the public and private sectors, or solely by the private sector.

(Deng, 1980)

Following the release of Deng's directive, the State Council issued the first formal policy statement on Housing Reform in 1982. In this simple directive China unveiled two decades of housing reform programme. Thus far, students of Chinese housing reform have been prone to exaggerate the importance of the housing reform process and many studies have largely sought to describe only specific policies (Chu and Kwok, 1990; Chiu and Lupton, 1992; Choko and Chen, 1994; Wang and Murie, 1996). Few have attempted to view housing reform from the perspective of a macro socio-economic transformation of the socialist welfare society. It is argued in this chapter that housing reform is but one element in the inter-linked set of radical socio-economic changes that needs to be made. The distinction of the housing reform process, however, lies in the fact that it requires institutional, legal and financial arrangements which are more demanding than most other reforms. Likewise, the dual nature of housing both as a consumption good and an investment asset makes the implementation of housing reform more complex. The commodification process of housing involves much more than a simple transfer of ownership. On the one hand, it is part of the national economic reforms with the aim of improving people's living environment; on the other hand, it is also part of a wider social re-organization process defining anew who should get what from housing. This process will have a serious impact on the existing pattern of resource distribution. Questions of distributive justice have never been seriously attempted. The experimental nature of many reform policies has also encouraged a strange breed of public management, frequently giving rise to charges of mismanagement and even corruption. Many housing reform failures were at the same time the inevitable result of hasty policies and clumsy policy transfers.

This chapter will examine three areas: (a) the development of housing reform since 1979; (b) the impact of the housing reform process, in particular the question of housing inequality, segregation and social costs; and (c) the question of sustainability, where the institution of the Housing Provident Fund (HPF) will be discussed. Analyses and illustrations of the three themes will largely draw on empirical data collected during field trips to Shenzhen, Shanghai and Guangzhou, the three Chinese cities with the highest per capita GDP (27 005 yuan, 22 275 yuan and 22 200 yuan respectively in 1996[1]) in the period 1994–98. The historical review will focus more on the early trajectory of housing reform since 1979, particularly the failure of rent and wage reforms. The section on social cost will examine social inequality, segregation, housing affordability and land shortages for public sector housing as a result of the change process. The question of sustainability is perhaps the very core of the whole reform process. Many cities experienced success at the beginning of the reform but soon suffered varying degrees of failure. How to make the reform sustainable is perhaps the most theoretically intriguing and practically challenging issue for students of housing reform. Here we shall examine the experiences of the Singaporean-modelled HPF in Guangzhou and Shanghai. We shall argue that the degree of marketization in some ways determines the necessity of the HPF institution and its usefulness as a housing finance institution.

The development of housing reform

The main concern in this chapter is urban housing reform since families in rural areas provide their own housing. (Eighty per cent of the population live in rural housing. Per capita floor space of residential buildings in rural areas was 21.7 square metres in 1996, which was much higher than the 8.5 square metres in urban areas.[2]) Work units and housing bureaus supply the largest fraction (75 per cent) of urban housing (Lau, 1993). Under socialist ideology, public sector housing provision formed part of the socialist welfare system. Housing provision, especially for state employees, was a responsibility of the state. Between 1949 and 1990, 1.98 billion square metres of housing was built in Chinese cities and towns: 1.73 billion square metres (87 per cent) by the public and collective sectors and only 0.25 billion square metres (13 per cent) by individual families (private) (Wang and Murie, 1996). Between 1949 and 1978, private home-ownership was criticized as a capitalist tendency. In order to provide the necessary housing for the expanded public-sector workforce in the state economic development planning system, housing investment was planned alongside other capital investment as an integral part of a development project. As a result, house-building, distribution, maintenance and management were decentralized to each public institution, rather than to a unitary housing authority. Access to housing was based on the employment status of the household head and assessed by government-determined standards, rather than need as in welfare capitalist systems.

Very low rents have been charged since 1949. Between 1949 and 1990, rent in most Chinese cities accounted for only 2–3 per cent of total household income (Wang and Murie, 1996). In 1997, the average rent per square metre in the 35 large and medium-sized cities was 1.29 yuan, which was 20 per cent of the cost rent or 12 per cent of the market rent of comparable housing units. On average, rental charges account for only 4 per cent of the income of two-earner households (Li, 1997). In the 1980s, the state paid 5–6 billion yuan to subsidize housing maintenance each year. However, public sector housing on the whole has been in a state of poor maintenance due to insufficient rental revenue to finance proper maintenance works. On top of this, there are other problems pertaining to a public-sector dominated housing system: for example, inequalities and unequal access, corrupt practices during allocation, and so on (Lau, 1993; Wang and Murie, 1996).

In the following section, a summary of the developmental stages of urban housing reform up to 1994 as outlined by Wang and Murie will be presented, followed by a discussion on the post-1994 housing monetarization policy.

The first housing reform experiment, 1979–81

Xian and Nanning were the two cities selected for the first housing reform experiment in 1979. In Xian, the selling price was based on the basic building costs of the total floor space of newly completed buildings: only 18 of 39 flats were sold to 15 families (eight families paid the full amount and seven families had chosen to pay by instalments over five years). At the national level, 60 different cities and towns all over the country carried out similar experimental schemes. The cost of a typical housing unit was equivalent to about 10–20 years' salary at that time. Demand for house purchase was low because (a) the price was too high relative to income and current rent; and (b) the mortgage repayment period was too short (only limited to five years) and most people could not afford the mortgage and wanted to repay the loan over a longer period. The first experiment was abandoned in 1982 due to low demand for these newly completed housing units (Wang, 1992).

The second experiment, 1982–85

New pilot tests of commercialization for urban housing were carried out in four cities: Zhengzhou (in Henan), Changzhou (in Jiangsu), Siping (in Sichuan) and Shashi (in Hubei). Under this scheme, individual purchasers paid one-third of the total construction cost (replacement cost) of a residential unit while the government and the purchasing work unit provided an equal share of the outstanding balance. The heavy burden on the work units and the government provoked many complaints. Similar provision was given in 160 cities and 300 county towns.

This experiment was different from the previous one: (a) purchasers were not required to pay the full purchase price of the housing unit; (b) apart from buying newly-completed flats, existing public tenants could buy the flats they occupied; and (c) it was accompanied by an additional proposal to change the context of the wage system and to increase rent in publicly-owned houses. Property rights were to be shared between the purchaser and the work unit. The property could change hands through inheritance or family division. However, individuals had no right to sell or rent the property in the open market and if they no longer needed the house, it had to be returned to the original seller (that is, the work units or housing bureau). A proportion of the original price would then be paid to the household. With a low rent system and without the prospect of capital gain, demand for home purchase was low. The experiment ended in 1985.

The third experiment, 1986–88

To coordinate and direct housing reform, the State Council set up a Housing Reform Steering Group in 1986. Housing Reform Offices were also set up at city level. The Housing Reform Steering Group proposed a strategy to raise rent (and introduce housing subsidy) and to promote sales of public-sector housing (old and new). The third housing reform experiment started in Yantai (Shandong) in 1987 and the entire process of housing production, distribution and consumption was to be commercialized. The long-term goal was to establish a housing market in which the state and other employers would have no direct distribution functions in housing. Through the reform, housing distribution would be changed from material distribution to monetary distribution. It was planned that, after the reform, people would only obtain housing of a size they could afford.

The main methods tried out in Yantai included the following: (a) increasing rent in the public sector to the level which could cover the standard cost; (b) issuing special housing subsidy coupons which had a value equal to Chinese currency but which could only be used for public sector housing consumption. This measure was considered necessary due to the low wage system. Employees affected by rent increase would need the subsidy to compensate for the loss arising from the increase in rental charges. In the state planners' minds, housing subsidy was to be gradually phased out after salaries had been increased to a level sufficient to meet family housing costs. The other main methods were (c) encouraging public sector tenants to buy the houses they occupied at standard sale prices; and (d) to set up housing funds and a housing savings bank. Up to 1988, the Yantai plan was reported as successful and most of its elements were later incorporated into the central government's post-1998 housing reform policies.

The National Housing Reform Plan, 1988

The National Housing Reform Conference held in 1988 confirmed that housing reform could bring about great economic and social benefits and resolved to effect its overall implementation. The overall objective of the reform was to realize housing commercialization according to the principles of the socialist planned market economy. Housing reform was seen as part of a wider economic system reform. Housing reform was also linked to reforms in salary and distribution systems, the finance and tax systems, and the development planning system.

Two major approaches were recommended: (a) rent increase (or the issue of housing subsidy coupons to offset rent increases); and (b) the sale of public sector housing (the sale price to include building costs and land compensation costs). A new housing distribution system was set up whereby new public sector housing would be put up for sale first and if there were 'left-over' dwellings, they would then be allocated as public rental units. It was proposed to bring all cities and towns into the reform programme within three years. However, rising inflation in late 1988 and political unrest in 1989 slowed down the housing and economic reform programmes in the following years.

In a large country such as China, some variation in practice is common. Among different cities, therefore, the exact nature of housing reform varied. In some cities, rent increases were balanced out by the issue of housing coupons; in other cities, step-by-step rent increases were not accompanied by the issuing of housing coupons/rent allowance/subsidy. Some required new tenants to pay a deposit while some did not. In most cities, the method of a sale price with substantial discounts available according to the number of years' service in the work unit was adopted, and the practice was generally welcomed by eligible workers. In 1991, Shanghai implemented its housing reform programme, which included: (a) establishing a compulsory housing savings system (*zhufang gongjijin*, or housing provident fund); (b) increasing rent and issuing housing coupons; (c) requiring new tenants of public-sector housing to pay a large deposit; (d) providing discounts for house purchase; and (e) establishing a Shanghai Housing Authority to carry out housing reform.

Urban Housing Reform Resolution, 1991

Five specific aims were stated in the 'Urban Housing Reform Resolution 1991' for the 1991–95 Eighth Five Year Plan period: (a) to restructure rents to enable basic housing reproduction (to cover costs for basic construction, maintenance, repair and management); (b) to solve over-crowding problems (those with per capita living floor space of less than four square metres); (c) to eliminate dangerous housing; (d) to increase per capita living floor space to 7.5 square metres by 1995 and ensure the proportion of appropriately designed unit housing (self-contained and non-dormitory type) would reach 40–50 per cent; and (e) to ratio-nalize and standardize continuous housing investment to sustain hous-ing construction. By the year 2000, (a) rents in the public sector would be increased to a level which would cover basic construction and main-tenance costs plus investment interest and property tax; (b) the average floor space per person should reach 8 square metres, and the propor-tion of independent and self-contained housing units out of the total housing units would reach 60–70 per cent; and (c) commercial prop-erty development and finance systems would be established. State housing provision was to be replaced by commercialized housing after 2000. Each local government was encouraged to produce its own reform plans to suit its local social and economic conditions. The price of flats for sale was kept at a very low level so as to gain support from work unit employees. This in turn undermined the idea of a healthy circulation of housing capital. The State Council suspended low price sales in late 1993.

The State Council's housing reform decision, 1994

The 'Decision on Deepening the Urban Housing Reform', published by the State Council Housing Reform Steering Group in 1994, included seven major aspects, as set out below:

1. A change in the housing investment system (a reasonable share of housing costs to be borne by the state, local government, work unit and the individual).
2. A change in the housing management system (socialized housing provision and management by specialized non-governmental bodies).
3. A change in the housing distribution system (from material distribu-tion to monetary distribution). To do this, the salary system also

had to be reformed. Housing allocation was to take into account income of households. High-income families (those who could afford to purchase a two-bedroom apartment from the market at 5–6 times the annual family income) were asked to satisfy their housing need by purchasing market price housing. In the sale of public sector housing, a price based on costs[3] would be applied to low- and middle-income families. A standard price, which took into consideration costs and affordability, was proposed as a transitional mechanism if the basic cost price caused financial difficulties.[4]

4. The establishment of a dual housing provision system in which there would be supplies in social and commercial housing. The former would provide *jingji shiyong zhufang* (economic and suitable housing, sometimes known as *anju gongcheng*, peaceful living projects) to middle- and low-income households, whilst the latter would provide housing for the high-income families.

5. The establishment of a compulsory savings system for housing, the Housing Provident Fund (with a typical 5 per cent contribution from employees and 5 per cent contribution from employers[5]).

6. The establishment of housing insurance, finance and loan systems which would enable both policy-oriented and commercial developments.

7. The establishment of a healthy, standardized and regulated market system of property exchange, repairs and management.

It was hoped that by the year 2000, rents would be increased to the level of roughly 15 per cent of a working couple's total salary. Statistics, however, showed that rent increases were well below this target. In late 1997, the average rent to a two-earner household was only 4 per cent of their income.

Housing monetarization, 1998

Despite two decades of work, urban housing reform is still making limited progress. One major stumbling block is the continued practice by work units of allocating heavily subsidized welfare housing in kind in most cities. In March 1998, Premier Zhu Rongji declared that from the latter half of 1998 onwards, work units should stop such practices and housing subsidy would be monetarized: that is, either paid to workers in a one-off lump sum or as monthly instalments for a period up to 20–25 years. Work units were allowed to include this monetarized housing subsidy in workers' monthly remuneration or deposit it into workers' Housing Provident Fund individual accounts, from where it may be withdrawn to purchase housing or pay for higher rental charges. Monetarized housing allocation is regarded a breakthrough measure that can speed up urban housing reform. It is hoped that a general increase of consumer housing subsidy will enhance housing consumers' ability to pay for *jingji shiyong zhufang* (economic and suitable housing) (Li, 1997). After the introduction of a monetarized housing allocation system, it was intended that workers would stop relying on work units for welfare housing allocation. The accumulated housing subsidy being monetarized can then be used to pay for the purchase of economic and suitable dwellings.

Differential practices prevail in different cities due to varied financial circumstances. Shunde, one of the richest cities in Guangdong Province in the Pearl River Delta region, started to implement the monetarized housing allocation system for staff in government departments, schools and hospitals in January 1994. In Guangzhou, the capital of Guangdong province, new staff joining the 230 work units of government departments or agencies after 29 September 1997 received monetarized housing subsidy. Those employed before that date could opt to remain in the old welfare housing allocation system. Monthly housing subsidy in 1998 ranges from 233 yuan (general grade staff) through 467 yuan (Section Chief) up to 933 yuan (City Major and equivalent grade). It is paid over 25 years into the employee Housing Subsidy accounts under the management of the Guangzhou Housing Provident Fund Management Centre. Staff in receipt of monetarized housing subsidy are no longer eligible for buying or renting heavily subsidized welfare housing. Assessed market rents or prices will be charged if they rent or purchase welfare housing. In Shandong province, government staff employed before 31 December 1997 receive lump sum compensation in lieu of housing in kind. Years of service, rank and entitled housing space are all taken into account when calculating the level of cash compensation. Those joining government service after 1 January 1998 have their housing subsidies included in their monthly remuneration (that is, about 25 per cent of basic wages).[6]

Apart from this monetarized housing allocation system, a series of new measures will be introduced to facilitate a market in residential housing. Market housing is expected to become the growth point for the national economy. Urban housing system reform has been designated as one of the five priority reforms of the new government under Premier Zhu. New measures within the urban housing reform will help institutionalize a secondary market for the public sale of flats and market housing to promote the active circulation of commodified housing.

Ways will be sought to reinforce legislative programmes on housing provident funds. Moreover, more funds will be injected to help create a housing mortgage market to make home purchase more affordable. The rent reform target by the year 2000 is intended to increase rents to a level equivalent to 15 per cent of the income of a two-earner household. Economic and suitable housing projects will continue.

According to the report made by State Councillor Li Teiying in late December 1997, progress was noted in five areas after the implementation of the urban housing system reform programmes. First, housing provident funds had been set up across the 36 large and medium-sized cities and 213 regional and county level cities in all 31 provinces, autonomous regions and municipalities directly under the central government. The establishment of housing provident funds is regarded as the foundation of the new urban housing system. About 80 billion yuan were deposited into HPFs. In cities such as Shanghai and Nanjing, 95 per cent of employees had joined the fund as depositors. Work has just been started on introducing legal regulatory measures on the management of housing provident funds. Such funds are regarded as an important source of funding to finance home purchase and house-building activities. Among the 35 large to medium-sized cities, many had started to make use of housing provident funds to provide home mortgage loans. About 14 per cent of HPF loans were used by individual home purchasers. Up to September 1997, the Shanghai HPF had provided 3.8 billion yuan in loans to 60 000 eligible families.

Second, rent reform, though making limited progress, had pushed up the rent to income ratios in some cities. On average, public rent stayed at 0.8–1.8 yuan per square metre. Among the 35 large to medium-sized cities, public sector rentals on average reached 1.29 yuan per square metre. In Shenzhen, Daqing and some medium and small cities, cost rents had been effected.

Third, as a result of the policy on the sale of public sector flats, the owner-occupation rate had also gone up. With the exception of Beijing and Tianjin, over 50 per cent of saleable public flats were sold to workers. In some provinces (such as Guangxi, Guangdong, Hunan, Shanxi, Zhejiang and Henan), over 80 per cent of saleable public flats were sold. Home ownership rates in the latter two provinces reached 70 per cent.

Fourth, new approaches to urban housing reform were tried out in different cities. The cost of housing production had been taken into account when the Nanjing and Tianjin municipal government allocated public sector housing to eligible staff, and the practice of 'free' or 'nominal charge' housing allocations was terminated. In Shanxi province,

housing allocation had been monetarized in all government departments and institutions, and housing (new and old) had been sold at
cost price without discounts. In Shandong province, the monetarized
housing allocation system was implemented by phases within government departments and party organizations in 1998. Similar arrangements
had been made for Guangzhou city government staff.

Fifth, *anju gongcheng* (comfortable living housing projects, or peaceful living projects) were first implemented in 1995 to demonstrate the
government's concern over the housing affordability problem of low-
income households. Tax exemptions, fee reduction and land grants at
concessionary rates had reduced the cost of housing production of the
anju housing. A centralized production of *anju* housing (termed socialized housing production) had replaced the uncoordinated housing
construction by individual work units in some cities. Purchasers of *anju*
housing had to pay the cost price for purchasing their homes. Between
1995 and 1997, 650 000 households benefited from the scheme. *Anju*
projects providing economic and suitable housing to low-income
urban dwellers are often described as housing with social security
programme characteristics.

The impact of housing reform

The above provides a sketch of the positive aspects of the urban housing reform. In the following paragraphs, the social costs of implementing the urban housing reform programmes will be examined. These are
grouped under two major themes: (a) housing inequality and segregation; and (b) the social cost of housing marketization.

Housing inequality and segregation

Housing inequality is not unique to socialist China: there are also
reports of gross housing inequality in the Eastern European countries
(Chapman and Murie, 1996). The problem of housing inequality in
urban China is exacerbated by the occupational welfare system whereby
housing-in-kind benefits vary according to the status of the employers.
State Councillor Li Teiying commented that on average housing conditions of staff employed in government departments and party institutions were generally better than those of other employees. However,
the rates of rent increase among them were much lower than generally
expected because the earnings of government and party employees
were usually lower than those of employees in profit-making enterprises. Government and party employees' generous housing allocation

standards with low rents/prices were criticized as setting a bad example which, in turn, held up changes in urban housing reform (Li, 1997). In the process of implementing the housing reform measures, some privileged groups benefited more than others. There is clear evidence that inequitable housing allocation practice has not yet been removed after housing reform. The example of the Shenzhen case study can confirm this.

In Shenzhen, the housing issue is complicated by the fact that many employers are overseas investors employing thousands of temporary residents as workers and providing less than desirable housing. A dormitory housing unit for 6–8 workers in double-bunk beds is the norm for most migrant workers. For those with family members (wife and husband both working and child being looked after by grandparent living with the family) in Shenzhen, they usually have to spend up to half of their income on renting private accommodation as employers usually do not provide housing for migrant workers' family.[7]

Shenzhen City Housing Bureau, the public sector housing authority, is charged with the responsibility of providing welfare housing to employees (with permanent resident status) of government departments/institutions, and selected state-owned enterprises accorded priority for receiving support. In 1993 the Housing Bureau also started a *wei li* (low-profit) housing programme. Low-profit housing is mainly built for employees of municipal agencies, or state-owned enterprises, or enterprises with 50 per cent or more shares owned by the state. Employees of the following approved enterprises and agencies are also eligible: enterprises using highly-advanced and new technology, export-oriented enterprises, enterprises providing daily vegetables and foods, civil affairs agency-sponsored enterprises, public utilities companies and property management agencies.[8]

In terms of the opportunity for obtaining adequate housing at a subsidized price or rent, clearly government workers and those eligible for welfare housing are far better off than others. Other than paying less (at below-cost price or rent), they are normally allocated a welfare housing unit in a housing estate with adequate community facilities within two years of their employment in Shenzhen, while other employees are only eligible for *wei li* (low-profit) housing, which is more costly than welfare housing. The average price for welfare housing in 1997 was 1000 yuan per square metre, while prices for low-profit housing were set at 2500–3500 yuan per square metre. Similarly, rental charges for welfare housing in 1997 were only 5.5–7.9 yuan per square metre whereas, for low-profit housing, rental charges were three times those of welfare housing (set at 18–20 yuan per square metre) (*Fangdichan Kuaixun*, 6, 1998). Housing inequality is reflected in the fact that eligible applicants of *wei li* housing may not be earning as much as the government workers, and neither were they guaranteed housing allocation within two years. They also have to pay more for the purchase or renting of low-profit housing. Waiting for a much longer period for the allocation of a more costly and less desirable low-profit housing unit (usually in high-rise housing blocks requiring more expensive management and maintenance fees), employees of enterprises are placed in an inequitable position when compared with government staff.

One often mentioned explanation is that government workers are not so well paid as people working in enterprises. It may be true in some cases, but statistics show that in recent years the average annual wage of employees in the state sector has been higher than that of other employees (Shenzhen City Statistical Bureau, 1995). Moreover, their real wage (wage after discounting the effect of inflation) grew faster (7.2 per cent per annum) than that of average wage earners (6.7 per cent per annum) during the period 1979 to 1994 (Shenzhen City Statistical Bureau, 1995). In the eyes of the general public, it is questionable for the government employees to continue to receive favoured treatment in housing provision, such as purchasing public sector housing below cost and with subsidized interest rates.

Housing segregation is not a new phenomenon in China. In the imperial era, there was evidence of housing segregation when the privileged class lived within the emperor's walled city boundary and housing for the poor was built outside the city wall. Such segregation became less visible after the Communist Party assumed power and took to provide housing as an in-kind occupational welfare for workers irrespective of rank. However, as the socialist market economy takes shape, housing segregation becomes more apparent.

An empirical study of the Shekou Industrial Area of Shenzhen's SEZ completed in 1995 has confirmed the emergence of housing segregation in the socialist market economy (X. Liu, 1995). There are clear signs that people belonging to the very rich, professional and managerial class are residing in some areas of market housing blocks or bungalows physically segregated from the rest, while the low-pay manual migrant workers (mostly single persons) are living in areas near the factories where dormitory-type housing units of minimum standards are built. There is sub-standard housing of a temporary nature for temporary residents who are either not provided with housing by their employers or are too poor to pay for private rented housing and therefore have resorted to squatting on hillsides or in construction sites. Workers belonging to one other group – government or state-owned enterprises' employees – who have been given public sector housing units (rented flats or sale flats) are luckier than the temporary residents as they only pay below-cost housing rent or prices for adequate housing of a high quality located in a well-planned community. Many public housing estates built and managed by state-sponsored agencies in Shenzhen have been awarded commendation certificates for their high quality by the central government authority.

The emphasis on building market housing which is basically used to accommodate the privileged few (the rich, professionals or the managerial elite) and the exclusion of a majority of the temporary residents from public sector housing has further reinforced the problems of housing segregation. The dormitory-type housing blocks and temporary housing areas can be easily identified by their unattractive outer appearances. Many of them are not properly maintained and marks of dilapidation can be found on the walls and other common areas, such as public corridors and staircases.

Social costs

The development of market housing has, on the one hand, provided a new source of finance to government, but on the other hand it has created new social problems. Needs of the poor are neglected as housing becomes less affordable. In the housing marketization process, the emphasis placed on building market housing for sale is obvious. Throughout the years, market housing production has constituted a major share of all residential housing[9] completed in Shenzhen, the Chinese city with the highest per capita GDP. The share of market housing out of the total residential housing built ranges between 58 per cent and 95 per cent during the period 1980–94. Out of the total construction space of 18 805 200 square metres of residential housing built between 1980 and 1994, 13 814 500 square metres (73.46%) were built as market housing (Lau, 1997).

A similar situation occurred in Guangzhou. From 1991 to 1995, out of 14 781 300 square metres of residential housing completed, 55 per cent was market housing (G. Zhang, 1996). During the following five-year plan period (1996–2000), market residential housing will constitute 60 per cent of the total constructed space (18 600 000 square metres, or 310 000 dwelling units). Market housing dominance in both Shenzhen and Guangzhou does not adhere to the guiding principle set by the State Council Housing Reform Office, which stated that 70–80 per cent of residential housing should be economic and comfortable housing units sold at cost or low-profit basis and targeted at the middle-income households, 15 per cent should be market residential housing built for high income households, and the remaining 5–15 per cent should be low-cost housing for low-income households.[10]

The housing affordability problem

The problem of property price rises in major cities in the early 1990s has created a new housing affordability problem for enterprises which rely on market housing to accommodate their employees. For instance, in 1988 in Shenzhen, multi-storey market housing was available at an average price of 900 yuan per square metre of construction space, the ratio of market price to the multi-storey welfare housing price (397 yuan) being 2.27 to 1. But in late 1993, market housing has increased to 6550 yuan per square metre while welfare housing stayed at 524 yuan per square metre, with the ratio changing to 12.5 to 1.[11] The disparity in prices of market and welfare housing and the rapid increase in market housing price induced a higher demand for public sector housing for which the Shenzhen Housing Bureau has not been given adequate resources.

The price increase in the market-housing sector is thought to be irrational and not working according to the market principle of genuine demand and supply. Demand was boosted by the actions of work units (basically state-owned enterprises which used government money to purchase market housing units to meet the housing needs of their employees: Dong, 1995). Various research studies have confirmed one significant finding, namely that market housing is not built only for affluent individuals; many market housing units are purchased by resourceful work units and then allocated as welfare rental housing or sold to eligible employees at a heavily-subsidized price. One source has suggested that between 1985 and 1992, almost 60 per cent of the market residential housing on sale in Guangzhou was purchased by work units (Fu, 1994). Another source suggests that with the exception of 1993, almost half of the market residential housing on sale in Guangzhou City proper was bought by work units during the Eighth Five Year Plan period (1991–95) (G. Zhang, 1996).

Nation-wide statistics on vacant residential property have shown that there were 52 500 000 square metres in late 1997 (*Beijing Economic Daily*, 13 June 1998). In Shenzhen, 1 919 100 square metres of residential flats were found to be vacant in mid-1997 (Zhang *et al.*, 1997).

According to the Guangzhou City Information Centre on Housing and Real Estate, the vacancy rate of market dwellings on sale between January and October 1996 was high. In the urban centre, 11.4 per cent of dwellings on sale were vacant, whilst in the suburban areas, the vacancy rate rose to 20.1 per cent.[12] Real estate development companies therefore had to bear a heavy bank interest burden. As the banks were unable to recoup the building loans on time, other industries or business sectors in need of loans for development would also be affected because the building loans were tied up. This had a negative impact on the normal functioning of the national economy. Such demand has not been supported by genuine individual consumers' purchasing power and therefore will have to change rapidly when the work units' fund for market housing purchase dries up.

In 1995, 36 per cent profits were recorded among housing and real estate companies in Shenzhen compared to the nation-wide average profit margin of 12 per cent.[13] In Guangzhou, the insistence on having a high profit margin (normally over 20 per cent and sometimes up to 40 per cent) is considered another important factor behind the inflated property prices there. Excessive profit pursued by property developers is one of the factors pushing up prices, which in turn makes market housing unaffordable. High prices are also attributed to the numerous taxes and charges (85 types in Guangdong) and the expenses incurred in the construction of community facilities (such as clinics, food stalls, filling stations and restaurants). In the process of housing marketization, property developers, government departments and agencies chase after maximum benefits while consumers suffer high prices.

Land shortage for public housing

The actual benefit of selling land for housing and real estate development is obvious. There are substantial revenues from land sales. These are used for speeding up the infrastructure development. For example, land in better locations in Shenzhen had been earmarked for sale to develop market housing since the late 1980s, and land allocated to the Shenzhen Housing Bureau for the construction of low-profit housing or public rental housing for temporary residents was often in remote and inaccessible sites which require more expensive financial investment for infrastructure development. Due to the high cost of construction, some sites allocated to the Shenzhen Housing Bureau to build high-rise housing blocks as early as in 1993 still stood idle in early 1996, despite the high demand for public sale flats.[14]

Maximization of land usage has recently become an agenda item of the land and housing authorities. This is in anticipation of the rapid population growth in the context of a relatively fixed and limited supply of land in major cities. As the land authority is more conscious of land use for public sector housing, there is a tendency to push the housing authority to construct high-density housing estates in order to economize on land use. Building high-rise residential housing blocks will be an option but it is an expensive one. Comparing like with like, the cost of constructing a housing unit in a high-rise housing block is 2.5–3 times that of a multi-storey housing block (Dong, 1994). Consequently, home purchasers will have to pay a higher price. Other than the cost of purchase, management fees are also higher for high-rise blocks.

Interviews with officials of the Shenzhen Housing Bureau have confirmed that there was a severe shortage of land for public housing, and even if land had been allocated, granting of approval for construction to go ahead was usually very late. This put the Housing Bureau in a very difficult position, as it had to rush to meet the building targets.[15] There were also worries that hurrying through the planning, design and construction stages would result in unsatisfactory building quality.

Housing Provident Fund: the question of sustainability in housing finance

One of the key concerns of housing reform in recent years is whether or not it is sustainable. Two levels of meaning can be discerned from this. The first addresses itself directly to the financial sustainability of housing reform. Many cities have experienced situations where local governments lack the necessary funding to complete new housing projects. Even when there are funds for construction, workers currently are paying subsidized rents or prices, and it would be an immensely difficult task for any government or work unit to take away the existing housing benefits from the recipients. This is apparently a less than ideal situation. Housing reform actually hastens the depletion of housing investment and hence results in the very unfair distribution of scarce housing resources. Therefore, in order to alleviate the problems of housing finance and sustainability, two major policies were implemented in the 1990s: HPF and the monetarization of housing. HPF is modelled on Singapore's Central Provident Fund, but is concerned only with housing contributions. At present, 36 cities in China have some form of HPF, with Shanghai claiming to be most successful and the first to adopt a full-scale HPF for its entire population. The monetarization of housing is a more recent policy which is aimed at enforcing a dividing line in 1998 to stop the distribution of welfare housing, meaning that from then on all housing subsidies would be in cash rather than in kind. Before the new policy has been fully launched, however, it has already triggered a scramble for the 'last through-train' for welfare housing.[16]

The second level of consideration in sustainability concerns a much broader shift in state policy for housing subsidies and cost sharing. Thus far housing allocation through work organizations in China is regarded as a form of welfare distribution. Allocated housing is regarded as part and parcel of the remuneration package. Since all workers are paid extremely low salaries, the state naturally assumes the full burden of housing production. To revolutionize this situation, the commodification process must re-evaluate the price of housing and decide who should eventually share the housing costs. The broad policy now adopted is the so-called '3 for 1' policy where the state, the work unit and the individual employee share the cost.[17] The latest housing monetarization policy thus involves the state increasing rent to distract people from public housing, selling public housing at discounted prices, and asking the work unit to provide a one-off subsidy for home purchase or to contribute a certain percentage of wages to the employee's home purchase fund. At the same time, this is augmented by the compulsory savings everyone has to deposit into the HPF. Even if all those measures do not result in affordability, the government has already instituted banking policies to allow for individual housing loans which were hitherto given only to work organizations and property development companies. In fact, in Shanghai the government is now prepared to reduce the loan ratio to state-owned enterprises and to shift from a policy of largely corporate lending to retail banking.[18]

The plethora of financial facilities/instruments all aim at a swift commodification. The question is whether these will be enough to boost the demand for home ownership. In the West, housing finance is but one facet of the housing system. The maturity of the housing market depends also to a great extent on people's perception of housing. But let us first examine the role played by the newly emerging financial institutions. The examples of Guangzhou and Shanghai Housing Provident Fund will be used to illustrate the related issues of sustainability.

The Housing Provident Funds in Guangzhou and Shanghai

The Guangzhou Housing Provident Fund, established in April 1992, is an additional source of finance to speed up residential housing construction projects to improve the housing conditions of the housing needy in Guangzhou. This is a compulsory savings scheme that offers low interest for account holders depositing money in, or borrowing money from, the Fund. However, those who have already purchased their own dwellings would lose out because the interest gained from the Fund is definitely lower than that of bank savings, in line with government policy.

In Guangzhou, the City Housing Provident Fund Management Centre is responsible for managing the Fund. It is financed by worker and employer contributions, each equivalent to 5 per cent of the worker's basic wages in the first three years of its operation. On average, 5 per cent represents a contribution of about 6 yuan per month by the worker and is roughly equivalent to 2 per cent of a worker's total wages.[19] The rate of contribution from both employees and the employers (the work units) stayed the same (that is, 5 per cent) for the period 1 June 1995 to 30 June 1997; but the basis of calculation was changed from the basic wages to the total wages. From 1 July 1997, more changes were introduced to the rates of contribution. From then onwards, the rate of contribution should take into account the wage levels of employees. Workers earning less than 500 yuan per month are required to contribute only 5 per cent of their basic wages and their employer contributes the same amount to the employee's housing provident fund account. For those with monthly earnings of 500–800 yuan per month, the rate of contribution stays the same (that is, 5 per cent) but is based on the total wages. For those earning more than 800 yuan per month, the rate is 7 per cent of total wages. The contributions plus the interest earned (interest rate is relatively low and is only equivalent to the savings rate generally offered by banks) are payable upon retirement or for purchase of subsidized or market housing. The Housing Fund is also used by the Guangzhou City Residential Housing Construction Office to build subsidized housing[20] for households in need of government assistance. Subsidized housing is exempt from land charges and some taxes. Completed flats can be sold or rented to Housing Fund account holders.

By the end of September 1997, 1.02 million employees (with resident permits) from over 6600 work units had joined the Guangzhou Housing Provident Fund. It is estimated that 90 per cent of the employees eligible for participation in the Fund have already joined. The amount of fund accumulated per month is over 50 million yuan. The total contribution accumulated in the Fund by the end of September 1997 was about 1631 million yuan.[21] State-owned enterprises suffering financial deficits were given approval by the government to defer joining the scheme. But from mid-1995 onwards, work units failing to join the Fund without approval were penalized. Their applications to sell their work unit flats to employees or use the work unit housing fund to maintain or improve their existing housing stocks were not processed by the housing authority. The penalty arrangement has been formalized and included in the 1997 Guangzhou City Housing Provident Fund Ordinance.[22]

Being the largest and the richest city in China, Shanghai sought to stand in the forefront of economic reform in the last two decades. The national housing reform movement, quite rightly, was spearheaded by Premier Zhu Rongji during his office as City Major in the early 1980s. HPF was a modification of the Singaporean model of Central Provident Fund with employee and employer contributions set at 5 per cent each. The Fund was set up in 1991. In 1997, the membership of HPF had grown to 4.36 million (covering 98 per cent of the working population in the metropolitan area of 7.5 million) and the fund level stood at 16 275 million yuan. The fund has, thus far, made loans to both work organizations and individuals amounting to 3010 million yuan, about 18 per cent of the fund. In addition, the fund also raised 159 million yuan through selling Housing Bonds as a supplement to general contribution.

Is the Housing Provident Fund a vehicle for sustainable housing finance?

Comparing Guangzhou and Shanghai, the former seems to be less dependent on HPF and its fund is managed less successfully. One reason is that the general wage level of Guangzhou is higher than that in Shanghai. With an even more open economy, residents of Guangzhou have more means to generate income than straightforward wages. Shanghai, on the other hand, is more dependent on HPF because Shanghai people have a comparatively lower wage level (the mean annual income is still 10 000 yuan). In the case of Shenzhen, its dependence on HPF[23] is almost negligible because people there enjoy the highest wages in the country and the banking system is more open.

No evaluation or assessment of HPF has been carried out so far in Guangzhou or in Shanghai as these funds have only been established for a few years. However, a number of observations or general concerns have been raised.

First, contributors to the Fund are bound to suffer some loss in light of the low interest gained. This is a direct consequence of the central government policy of low interest payments and low interest loans for borrowing from the Fund for home purchase or the house-building programme. Some bank experts have estimated that the loss of interest would be as high as 88.9 per cent. Their estimates were based on a comparison of the interest earned in HPF and the interest earned by putting the same amount of savings into a deposit account for 1 year.[24]

Second, there are also worries that the Fund is not fully utilized due to the difference in the interest charged on loans from the Fund and the interest from bank deposits.[25] As the latter is higher than HPF interest, it is very likely that managers of the Fund would be less keen to offer loans to homebuyers. Consequently the original objective of accumulating more housing fund for the expansion of the housing programme is defeated.

Third, despite then Vice-Premier Zhu Rongji's reminder in late 1995 that 'we must have a proper system of management and checks',[26] there are incidents of misuse of the Fund. Research findings by the China Academy of Social Science have shown that the proportion of loans borrowed from HPF for the purpose of individual house purchase or work units' housing construction was small. In some cities, loans borrowed from HPF were used for commercial activities not related to residential housing construction or purchase. Some of the loans were used for building government offices or for car purchase.[27] As the depositors or account holders of HPF have no legal rights to monitor the use of the Fund, it is likely that institutions of influence would be interested in borrowing money from the Fund since its charges are lower than commercial bank interest rates. Another report has confirmed the low proportion of HPF loans supporting individual home purchase. Up to May 1997, 19 per cent of loans from the Shanghai HPF were used for that purpose. The proportion in other cities is as low as 3–5 per cent.[28]

Finally, there are doubts about the ability of the Fund to solve the problem of lack of finance for urban housing construction and home purchase. In Guangzhou, assuming that the cost of production of each 'Ecomomic and Suitable Housing Project' dwelling is at the minimum price of 1900 yuan per square metre, building 13 000 dwellings[29] of 60 square metres each would require 14 820 000 yuan in one year. This is 2.5 times the total annual contribution of 600 million yuan to the HPF. If an average two-earner household (earning an average of 2043 yuan per month in 1996) contributes 7 per cent of its monthly income and the employer contributes another 7 per cent, the average contribution will be 286 yuan per month, or 3432 yuan per year. If this household has to rely on its HPF accumulation to pay the 30 per cent down payment for the purchase of a public dwelling priced at 114 000 yuan (1900 yuan × 60 square metres), it will take almost 10 years to save enough money for the down payment. It is therefore appropriate to conclude that HPF, at the existing rate of contribution, could only solve part of the problem of lack of finance among housing authority and individual home purchasers.

In sum, the experience of HPF as a vehicle for sustainable housing finance for both Guangzhou and Shanghai varies with the performance of the economy as well as the general income level of their residents. HPF could not be the sole agent for adequate housing finance. It has to be used in conjunction with other financial tools, such as ordinary bank loans. However, the greatest threat to successful housing reform is still the relatively low rent of public housing. Despite continuous rent reform, the rate and magnitude of rent increase still fall far below house prices.

Conclusions: de-collectivization and commodification

The central concern of housing reform in China is essentially about a changing system of income distribution. Housing as a scarce resource will no longer be allocated through the state system. The government seeks to reduce its load in housing provision; and the state will no longer be the sole provider of housing. This involves two distinct but related social processes: first, the de-collectivization of state housing production and consumption from work organizations and state bureaucracies to intermediate organizations separated from the state; second, through a process of commodification, or what is currently coined 'monetarization', housing is expected to change gradually from a unilateral transfer welfare good to a commodity for exchange. These processes involve not simply a transformation of existing structures and institutions; they also lead to a fundamental change in people's conception towards housing. While it is difficult to conclude at this stage whether housing reform in China has failed or succeeded, our examination of three of the more prominent cities (Guangzhou, Shenzhen and Shanghai) reveals a number of pertinent issues which merit more rigorous examination in both policy and practice.

First, uncoordinated development in housing production, wage reform and the still largely-prevalent welfare housing under existing work organizations have resulted in a rather truncated development in housing reform. While there is still an acute housing shortage in many areas, the vacancy rate of new houses remains high. Many state-owned enterprises are rather reluctant to adhere strictly to the rule of housing reform and have sought to play down its impact on individual work units. The recent proposal to terminate welfare housing sparked off a wave of home purchase by work units, which snapped up expensive private properties for transfer to workers at extremely low prices. This has been described by housing observers as trying to get on the 'last through-train' to welfare housing, in the light of the central government's proposal to terminate welfare housing from 1 July 1998.[30] In fact, as a result of the new housing reform proposal, as well as the national decision to reduce the number of state-owned enterprises in the next few years, the housing reform process has actually aggravated existing housing inequality.

Second, while institutional innovations such as HPF and the shift in housing loans from corporate banking to retail banking provide additional funding to facilitate home purchase and house-building, only a fraction of this money is actually used for home purchase by individuals. As a leader in housing reform with the best-organized HPF, Shanghai also encounters housing finance problems. House prices have gone up much faster than wage increases. In places such as Guangzhou and Shenzhen, where the degree of marketization and wage levels are comparatively higher, the dependence on HPF is still small. Even though the institution has been successfully established, at the present stage it acts only as one of the many savings institutions, providing an additional channel for the government to solicit investment finance.

Third, one of the key strategies used thus far is the promotion of home ownership through selling state rental housing at discounted prices. Many critics have suggested that state properties are in fact being transferred below cost (at about one-seventh of general construction cost per square metre: See Gong, 1997; Wang and Murie, 1998; X.Q. Zhang, 1998). The heavy emphasis put on housing reform policy by the central government in recent years has hastened this process of transfer. As a result, the transfer process is fraught with corruption, irregularities and malpractice. The end result is that those who were discriminated against in the old system might not be helped at all by the new system. Housing inequalities are perpetuated and aggravated, but in a different form. In addition, officials are often reluctant to differentiate social classes more scientifically and as a consequence scarce housing resources are allocated on the basis of status rather than need. It is not surprising that migrant workers become second-class citizens in the housing market while government workers continue to receive favourable treatment.

Finally, the whole housing reform structure has been based on the policy assumption that home ownership and marketization is the best way out of China's urban housing problem. State ownership and provision have been condemned as not being conducive to solving housing problems. The World Bank also gave high priority to the promotion of owner-occupation (Hamer, 1997). It has already been suggested elsewhere that home ownership is not what people care about most: it is the fear of continual rent increases that coerces people into home ownership (X.Q. Zhang, 1998). Some have even argued that what China needs is a reform of the housing delivery system rather than fundamentally commodifying the whole housing system when affordability and wage increases have not been able to keep pace with economic growth. Likewise, it has also been suggested that the reform policy in recent years has driven up land prices and construction costs. Overinvestment in housing and speculation, particularly housing at the high end, has been prevalent. The recent collapse of the Hong Kong housing market[31] is a vivid example of the adverse consequence of overinvestment in housing. It explains why critics have been arguing for a tenure neutral policy, rather than jumping on the bandwagon of home ownership and privatization. Perhaps the following quotation[32] from a Mr Zheng, a redundant worker from Beijing Capital and Steel Works, best encapsulates the sentiment:

> Now everybody in China no longer worries about food. What they worry about are house prices and housing reform. My sentiments on this are very complicated: on the one hand I think housing reform is good, but on the other I worry that I can never afford it. My wage is far too low. I only earn 714 yuan per month. If I want to buy a 60 square metre flat, now it's 5000 yuan per square metre. It will cost 300 thousand yuan. This figure is astronomical to me. How could I afford it?

Notes

1. *Statistical and Information Yearbook of Shenzhen 1997*, p.106; *China Statistical Yearbook 1997*, p.45; *Guangzhou Yearbook 1997*, p.57.
2. *China Statistical Yearbook* 1997, p.24 and p.291.
3. A price based on costs would cover seven cost elements including the costs of land acquisition and compensation, pre-construction costs (survey, design), building, neighbourhood public facilities, management, interest on loans, and tax.

4. The standard price includes two elements: affordable price (three years' total salaries for a couple is considered the affordable price for a new 56 square metre standard apartment); plus 80 per cent of housing savings including the employer's contribution over a period of 60 years in total (capped at 35 years for a male and 30 years for a female employee).

5. There is no standardized translation for this term. 'Housing Provident Fund' is sometimes translated as Housing Fund or Housing Accumulation Fund or Public Accumulation Fund. The rate of contributions varies in different Chinese cities.

6. *Nanfang Fangdichan (Southern Housing and Real Estate)*, 155 (April 1998), pp.9–10.

7. Data collected in field visits by Lau Kwok Yu in December, 1994 and 1995. Also see the report in *Apple Daily* (Hong Kong), 22 June 1995.

8. *Shenzhen Tequ Bao (Shenzhen Special Zone Daily)*, 5 October 1994.

9. Residential housing here refers to all public sector welfare low-profit housing and market housing built for residential purposes, but it does not include residential housing built by collectives and individuals in towns and villages within Shenzhen City.

10. *Nanfang Fangdichan (Southern Housing and Real Estate)*, No. 155 (April 1998), p.15.

11. Data collected in field visit by Lau Kwok Yu in January 1996.

12. *Yue Gang Xinxibao (Guangdong – Hong Kong Information Daily)*, 8 August 1997.

13. *Nangfang Fangdichan (Southern Housing and Real Estate)*, 139 (December 1996), p.19.

14. Data collected in field visit, January 1996.

15. Data collected in field visits by Lau Kwok Yu in September 1995 and January 1996.

16. 'The Urgency of the Housing Matters: Real Estate in Flame', *Yazhou Zhoukan (Asia Weekly)*, 1–7 June 1998, pp.14–15.

17. Shanghai Housing Provident Fund Management Centre (1996), *Shanghai Housing Provident Fund: Operation and Management*, Shanghai: Shanghai Popular Science, pp.15–24.

18. Besides the Construction Bank, the Commerce and Industry Bank, the Bank of China and the Agricultural Bank are now allowed to provide personal loans for home finance.

19. Guangzhou Housing System Reform Office (1992), *Guangzhou Fanggai Ziliao Xuanbian yu Wenti Jieda (A Selection of Information and Resources Plus Questions and Answers on Guangzhou Housing Reform)*, p.43.

20. Subsidized housing includes the '*Anju Project*' (Comfortable Housing Project). In Guangzhou, the first *Anju* Project was launched in Guangzhou in 1996.

21. Data supplied by Guangzhou Housing System Reform Office on 10 October 1997. Also see *Nanfang Fangdichan (Southern Housing and Real Estate)*, 145 (June 1997), p.39.

22. Guangzhou City Housing Provident Fund Ordinance (Clause 18), approved on 22 September 1997 and effective from 1 January 1998.

23. Less than 16 per cent of the total number of employees with permanent resident status in Shenzhen joined the Housing Provident Fund which is optional in nature. See Lau (1997), pp.17–19.

24. *Zhongguo Jianshebao (China Construction Journal)*, 4 June 1997.
25. *Zhongguo Jingyingbao (China Business)*, 3 June 1997.
26. Zhu Rongji (1995), speech delivered at a Seminar on National Housing Reform Experiences held on 15 December 1995.
27. *Zhongguo Zhengjuanbao (China Securities)*, 25 April 1997.
28. *Zhongguo Tudibao (China Land News)*, 20 May 1997.
29. The annual production target of Guangzhou Comfortable Housing Project for the period 1996–2000 is 13 000 dwellings at an average size of 60 square metres of construction space.
30. This was somehow postponed to the latter part of 1998. See *Ming Pao Daily News*, 17 July 1998.
31. There was a price drop of 40 per cent within 12 months after 1 July 1997 in Hong Kong's private domestic property market. The drastic price drop was subsequent to the rapid price rise of 75 per cent in the previous 18 months (January 1996 to June 1997). See http://www.info.gov.hk/rvd for details.
32. Wu (1998).

7
Conclusion

Bob Deacon, Ian Holliday and Linda Wong

In setting up the collection of studies presented here, the introduction made the point that Chinese social policy reform needs to be understood both in terms of its differences from change elsewhere and in terms of the global trends to which it conforms in some degree. Ample evidence of Chinese exceptionalism may be found in the chapters themselves. Indeed, these reveal a substantial diversity of experience even within China, as different regions and policy sectors pursue distinct reform trajectories. In a country as large as China, this is only to be expected. Nevertheless, several common themes do emerge, and provide the basis for comparative and theoretical analysis. This conclusion engages in both exercises. To begin with, however, it reviews the main themes of social policy reform in China.

Social policy reform in China

As the point of departure is the Maoist social policy system, our analysis must start by focusing on the changing nature of the employment contract. The social policy significance of state intervention in the labour market during the Maoist period was substantial. With the coming of economic reform, labour markets throughout China have been radically altered. In urban areas, workers are increasingly recruited by companies rather than being allocated to a position by the state, and now themselves possess some choice in where they work. Equally, employers can hire and fire in a far less restricted way, and are switching from lifetime employment to short-term contracts. Crucially, private-sector employers do not incur any obligation for workers' welfare, and the network of protection that used to centre on the company is gradually being deconstructed. Similarly, in rural areas the growth of the TVE sector means that village-owned factories and other production units can enter into employment relationships with other members of the village or with migrants from distant rural areas. These relationships are often similar to those established in towns by employers other than ministries, state entities and SOEs. They comprise a contractual agreement to buy and sell labour with no social protection obligations. In both urban and rural areas the transformation in social policy arrangements is radical.

In Chapter 2, Grace Lee analysed this critical dimension of reform by focusing on the way in which change in the labour market has disintegrated production and consumption. In an SOE much payment was in kind. SOEs built and managed housing, schools, colleges, clinics and hospitals for their workers. The SOE itself was under the control of the local party-state, as well as its parent ministry, and was indistinguishable from the state. It was, then, a 'welfare state' for its workers. Once this aspect of the SOE was withdrawn, whether because individual concerns were unable to meet their obligations or were replaced by other employers, the consumption of education, healthcare and pensions became detached from the employment relationship. Similar changes have taken place in rural areas with the shift away from collective farms. Before reform of the agricultural sector peasants would have obligations to produce their quota for the plan, but they would also have rights to services and social protection from the collective. Since reform was initiated, peasants have increasingly sold their produce at market prices, have perhaps employed (as owners of a collective TVE) migrants from other rural areas, and have had to make personal arrangements for education, healthcare and savings. The employees of a TVE have a purely market-based relationship with their employer. A key part of Lee's analysis is, however, her focus on problems that have constrained labour market reform in the past two decades, including inadequate policy design, bureaucratic inertia, managerial resistance and popular discontent. For these and other reasons, the transformation of social protection is not complete. Many workers and cadres in ministries, state institutions and a number of SOEs still have employment relationships that include mutual obligations and rights.

In Chapter 3 Linda Wong picked up the issue of how far welfare reform has progressed. She notes that the Chinese welfare system was never unified, being divided between the three major categories of urban workers, rural workers and the designated needy. She argues that major changes have been made to each system as competition and the cash nexus have swept through towns and villages. The underlying principle of the Chinese welfare system, she maintains, has switched from equality to efficiency, though the new principle is no easier to realize than was the old. Devolution of control and responsibility has also been a theme of the current changes. At the heart of reform efforts is an attempt to put in place a comprehensive social insurance system, covering pensions, unemployment, work injury and healthcare costs. This, in the reformers' terms, is 'socialization' of the welfare system. A key part of Wong's analysis is its international dimension. The Chinese reform process has taken place at least in part in response to international pressures. In overseeing reform, elite policy makers have made conscious efforts to learn from experience in other states. Since China was opened up to international agencies, many have sought to play a direct role in social policy reform. Like Lee, Wong examines the problems reform has encountered, including institutional blockages, a frequent lack of project champions, and financial constraints.

In Chapter 4, Anthony Cheung examined China's healthcare system, focusing on the critical issue of finance. Here too divisions in the pre-reform system are noted, since coverage for state employees was always better than that for urban workers, which in turn was better than that for peasants. Cheung argues that whilst the pre-reform system faced a series of problems, notably in the realm of funding, they were not the motor of change. Instead, economic change was the key to reform in this sector, as in so many others. He then surveys a series of experiments in reform of healthcare finance, noting the many problems that constrain change. These include the demographics of China's ageing population, the financial viability of new initiatives, and the supply-side resistance inherent in existing healthcare institutions. In a system in which markets for healthcare are emerging both at the luxury end of private clinics and at the near-destitute end of crude peasant deals, Cheung argues that healthcare provision is becoming a lot more unequal.

In Chapter 5 Ka-ho Mok focused on change in Chinese education. In the Maoist period education was provided freely by the state, and was also tightly controlled by it. In the post-Maoist period of 'socialist construction', the monolithic system has been deconstructed first by decentralization within the state sector and then by a shift towards 'multiple channels' of funding and a marketized education system. The major elements of reform are increased diversity, devolution, competition, choice and profit. Again the reform process is shown to be progressing at different speeds in distinct educational sectors. Again it is shown to be incomplete. As yet there are no true internal markets in Chinese education. However, the public–private distinction is being eroded by reform as private schools, colleges and universities emerge. The central themes of this chapter are the marketization that has swept over the Chinese educational system since the late 1970s, and the increased inequality that has come with it.

In Chapter 6 K.Y. Lau and James Lee analysed the process of housing reform that has taken place since the late 1970s. They argue that what started as a pragmatic response to housing problems experienced in the aftermath of the Cultural Revolution has become an increasingly ambitious set of changes. Their general theme is the progressive shift from collective consumption to individual responsibility that is currently taking place in China, as elsewhere. However, they go on to note that this is mainly an urban phenomenon, for in rural areas housing has always been provided chiefly by families. Again experimentation is a key element of reform, and problems – of inflation, political unrest, inequality and segregation – are highlighted. The international dimension to reform comes through very clearly in this chapter, with learning from elsewhere and the role of the World Bank prominent themes.

The clear impression given by these studies is that as reform progresses, individuals are moving away from the old 'iron rice-bowl' system of social protection to greater and lesser extents. In particular, members of the new elite, defined less by political status than by economic success, now make their own arrangements in the higher echelons of the markets for housing, education, healthcare and savings. At the other end of the social scale, an estimated 30 million floating workers drawn to the high-growth cities of the south and east are also disconnected from collective provision, and have little or no formal cover. Lacking membership of an SOE and also lacking the citizenship rights that flow from permission to live in a town or city, these people have no access to urban or state services. They provide for themselves and their families as best they can. At the lower end of China's emergent welfare markets, such provision as exists is most likely to take the form of privately-rented housing or dormitories, self-organized schools and a rough and ready market for medical care. In between these extremes, few (if any) people remain unaffected by the process of reform and the switch from a state collectivist to a more marketized system of welfare.

Chinese experience and comparative social policy analysis

The studies collected here do not and could not comprise a comprehensive analysis of social policy reform in China. Anything smaller than a multi-volume study cannot hope to do that. They do, however, survey the main themes of welfare change and thereby provide a basis for comparative analysis. At a time when the discipline of social policy is becoming increasingly focused on comparative questions, what observations can we draw from the Chinese experience presented here?

In seeking to answer this question, the first task is to decide with which other countries or regions it is sensible to make comparisons. Wong (1998) argues that the limited level of social protection provided by the MCA for marginalized individuals lacking work, family or other means of survival has to be understood within two key frameworks. One is the socialist focus on the workplace (*danwei*) as a source of social provision, and the other is the Confucian focus on the family and community as social support mechanisms. Looking north and west to post-Communist social policy reform in the former Soviet bloc must therefore be one point of comparison (Deacon, Hulse and Stubbs, 1997). Looking South and East to social policy development in the 'Confucian' welfare states of East Asia must be another (Jones, 1993; Goodman, White and Kwon, 1998). Is reformist China following in the footsteps of Eastern Europe or East Asia (McCormick and Unger, 1996)? But maybe things are not even this straightforward, for Eastern Europe is also taking lessons from elsewhere, including Western Europe and the USA. We need therefore to consider whether what can be discerned in the reform stories told here is the emergence of embryonic social citizenship rights, or alternatively a form of liberal individualism. At this point the agenda for comparative analysis becomes quite extensive.

Starting with a socialist perspective, the key task is not to draw the social policy comparisons with capitalist states that were of so much interest to Cold War observers, but to analyse the social policy impact of distinct transitions to market-based economic and political systems. Socialist states have long been held to outperform all others in managing the early stages of social policy development, generating excellent returns on standard welfare indicators such as life expectancy and literacy (Deacon, 1983; White, Murray and White, 1983; Doyal and Gough, 1991). They have tended to perform less well than capitalist states in the later stages of social policy development, seemingly exhausting the potential for welfare improvement in all spheres (except perhaps equity). Post-socialist social policy development is also patterned in this way. In the post-Soviet bloc liberalization and democratization have exacted a high social cost, evident in an increase in poverty and in decreases in life expectancy, school attendance and so on. In China, where liberalization has been managed by an undemocratic state, poverty continues to diminish and living standards are still rising.

There are signs of increasing regional diversity, and of threats to health standards in rural areas as the rural healthcare system collapses. Nevertheless, China had a good human development record in the past and continues to outperform its post-socialist counterparts today.

Trajectories of social policy change in post-socialist states reveal a number of patterns. In the post-Soviet bloc the high social cost of transition to a market economy has not prevented some countries from slowly reforming their social policy systems by drawing on some form of Western experience. In these states a tension between West European social market ideals embodying universal rights to social citizenship and a budget-induced, IMF/World Bank-backed privatization and residualization of social welfare has been evident in the 1990s and remains so today. Other countries in the region, particularly in the former Soviet Union, have made less progress towards economic reform and have experienced a prolonged period of extraordinarily high social cost. Here a combination of conservative attempts to preserve workplace welfare structures and economic difficulties has led to welfare collapse. In China, both scenarios are being played out. The extent of workplace welfare conservatism seen in some former Soviet states is also present in China (see Chapter 2). In the sphere of healthcare reform, an aspiration to universal citizenship rights in urban centres contrasts with marketization and individualization elsewhere (see Chapter 4). In housing, the decision of some enterprises to buy newly-built flats and provide them at a discount to their employees provides evidence of the continuing influence of the *danwei* model of social protection and of the many strands that feed into contemporary social policy reform (see Chapter 6). Because of the diversity of models being tried out in China, and because the conservatism of workers in rust-belt enterprises contrasts with the radicalism of workers in dynamic new sectors, it is very hard to determine the overall character of social policy reform.

The direct influence of external actors is possibly less great in China than in other post-socialist states. The World Bank has made a predictable contribution to the pension debate, arguing for a tiered policy comprising a basic pay-as-you-go scheme coupled with fully-funded individual accounts and no social pooling above the level that might be said to fit with a Confucian model of family provision (World Bank, 1997a). By contrast, it is also clearly concerned that health policy reform does not contain sufficient commitment to public health provision, especially in rural areas. However, the Bank, which has been a major player in many post-Soviet states, may be less influential in

China simply because of the sheer size of the place. Beyond this, the extent of China's reluctance to give up some of its controls on foreign investment, and its continuing non-membership of the World Trade Organization, mean that it is also protected from some of the policy shifts associated with globalization, such as a reduction in labour taxes. More generally, China seems to have a greater capacity to pick and choose from elsewhere than many other post-socialist states.

Turning to a 'Confucian' perspective, White (1998) notes that three broad positions on pension reform, and probably on social policy reform more generally, may be discerned among elite policy makers. The first, associated with the Ministry of Labour, is a socialist position emphasizing redistribution, wide social pooling and a large role for the state. The second, associated with the State Economic Structure Reform Commission, is a reform position emphasizing the role of private funds above the level of the basic state pension. The third, associated with elites in localities where new capital investment dominates, is a developmental statist position emphasizing the contribution of pension funds (whether state- or privately-managed) to economic growth. White (1998, p.185) claims that:

> what appears dimly to be emerging as the dominant policy paradigm is a form of state-led developmentalism along familiar East Asian lines, with the other two positions and their advocates as ideological outriders. As the new policy paradigm gains in strength, it is bringing China closer to its East Asian neighbours.

In this context the creation in April 1998 of a super Ministry of Labour and Social Security to take over the social security functions of the Ministry of Labour, Ministry of Personnel, Ministry of Civil Affairs, Ministry of Public Health and the State Economic Structure Reform Commission is interesting (see Chapter 3). It suggests that the outliers have been incorporated into a state-led developmentalist strategy. The implications of this reform for a social security policy which is still very varied at the local level is another matter. In Beijing, the financing of the healthcare system does not draw on contributions from workers and does not comprise individual accounts. This socialist policy orientation, associated with the Ministry of Health, contrasts with developments in some coastal cities, where the thinking of the State Economic Structure Reform Commission has influenced policy (see Chapter 4). The merged ministry may not be able to exercise its authority equally in all regions.

If White is broadly correct, the fate of Chinese social policy may therefore be bound up with the fate of social policy in the wider East

Asian region. On the one hand, the economic crisis caused by speculative short-term capital flows may damage the capacity of the Chinese government to offset problems in the rust-belt industries with the dynamism of the new capital sector. A scenario of post-Soviet welfare collapse is foreshadowed here. On the other, the increased concern on the part of the Asian Development Bank and other global actors that economies have in place an adequate social protection system to guard against the social and political consequences of market instability suggests that a state-led developmentalist approach to social policy with a role for compulsory savings and fully-funded pensions may prevail.

Chinese experience and Western theories of social policy change

In introducing this collection we noted that in the West the retreat of the state from social provision and the consequent redistribution of responsibilities between the market and civil society were initially brought under the umbrella term of privatization. We argued that possibly the most straightforward way of conceptualizing privatization in the social domain is as a reduction of the role of the state in social service provision, funding, and regulation (Le Grand and Robinson, 1984). Yet according to different writers, the term's contents can be quite elastic. Strategies such as de-nationalization, hiving-off, contracting-out, decentralizing responsibility, introducing fee-for-service provision and cost-recovery are commonly included. One consequence of this elasticity is that the Western focus on privatization gradually gave way to less pre-judgment of outcomes and more detailed interest in actual processes of change. The reforms that swept through public sectors in much of North America, Western Europe and Australasia in the 1980s and 1990s now tend to be grouped under the rubric of the new public management. The most significant shift is captured in the notion of a transformation of the state from provider to enabler, purchaser and regulator. Assessing Chinese experience in the context of the themes roughly sketched here generates a number of observations.

The first and most obvious point to emerge from this collection is that the debate about privatization that has rather faded from sight in the West is very much alive and kicking in China, whatever it is called. Each of the chapters brought together here addresses this issue in one way or another. Several aspects of the debates individual authors have with each other are worth highlighting. One is that, as Wong argues in Chapter 3, use of the term is certainly not current in China itself. It is loaded with rather too much capitalist meaning to be looked on with favour by the Party leadership, and is thought to imply selfishness and anti-social attitudes. Instead, terms such as marketization, commodification and monetarization are officially sanctioned. Second, it is clear from these studies that the Chinese case is by no means a simple instance of privatization. Services previously organized and provided by the state have not been shifted wholesale into the private sector. Instead, there is now a wide variety of institutional arrangements, many of which still intersect with the state in one way or another. So complex is the balance between individualism and collectivism that exists in contemporary China that a simple notion of privatization is not an adequate description. Third, the terms that tend to be favoured in many of the studies collected here are marketization, socialization or, occasionally, societalization, all of which are intended to capture the idea that 'non-state' is not necessarily the same as 'private', because of the intervening social variable. Fourth, however, it has to be said that privatization is actually in many ways a more accurate description of the Chinese case than of those in the West for which it was first invented. If we look at state involvement in the provision, financing and regulation of social policy, there has been a good deal more roll-back in China than in most (possibly all) Western states. In China, elements of social policy provision actually have been shifted from the public to the private sector, and whilst much of that provision has been picked up by 'society' in some way it is hard to see how, in the end, this does not count as privatization. One of the main reasons why such a dramatic and controversial term fits China better than it fits even Thatcherite Britain or Reaganite America is that the starting point was so much more statist in the Chinese case. Another reason is that real offloading of hitherto public-sector responsibilities actually has taken place in China to an extent unmatched in the West.

A second observation is consistent with the first. It is that the central new public management themes that dominate much social policy analysis in the West are not prominent in China. We must, of course, be careful about making generalizations about the West. The OECD (1995, p.25) has argued that responses by its member states to the pressure for public sector reform 'have many parts in common' and 'show a remarkable degree of convergence'. 'Taken together,' it maintains, 'the reforms represent a paradigm shift'. In support of these contentions, the OECD presented a checklist of eight common trends: devolving authority and providing flexibility; ensuring performance, control and accountability; devolving competition and choice; providing a responsive service; improving management of human resources; optimizing use of information technology; improving quality of regulation; and strengthening steering functions at the centre. Others, however, have begged to differ, arguing that '[c]ontrary to the official view taken by the OECD as an organization, there is no evidence of a linear homogenous trend in public sector development' (Naschold, 1996, p.2). In the end the OECD's position is unsustainable, for just as welfare states have the different pasts, presents and futures identified by Esping-Andersen and others, so reform of them is following distinct trajectories. The OECD's checklist nevertheless provides a useful general standard against which to measure contemporary Chinese reform. When we do this, what is most noticeable is that few elements on the OECD's list are visible in China. Even those that are present, such as devolving authority and providing flexibility or developing competition and choice, tend to describe very different processes of change in China and the West. This observation is consistent with the first because it reinforces the contention that the shift towards marketized provision has been more brutal and crude in China. Internal markets are a major theme of social policy change in the West. Full-scale exposure to markets is a more obvious theme in China. Moreover, the panoply of agencies, contracts and performance indicators that has emerged in some Western public sectors to substitute for market signals has no clear Chinese equivalent.

A third observation is that the international dimension to social policy change that is increasingly drawing the attention of social policy analysts can be studied in great depth in China. That dimension does not take the form of movement of some hitherto state functions to a supranational body such as the EU. In fact, in China since (and to some extent before) the 1978 reforms the shift has been in exactly the opposite direction, with a continental polity empowering its constituent provinces. Other aspects of international experience are, however, mirrored here. There has been clear policy learning and policy transfer, shown most clearly in this collection in the selective lessons drawn from Chile and, particularly, Singapore, in all sectors of social protection. The importance of Singapore as a model for Chinese social policy raises the intriguing question of whether China will begin to take on some features of what is sometimes called the 'East Asian welfare model' (White, 1998), but is better characterized as a productivist world of welfare capitalism in East Asia (Holliday, 1999). Certainly there is a clear productivist element to the current reform process. Beyond this, the role of international agencies, notably the World Bank, in contributing to social policy change comes through very clearly in this collection and provides grounds for further study. In particular, it makes possible comparison of the role of such agencies in China and the transition states of East-Central Europe, where work has already been undertaken (Deacon, 1997).

A fourth and final observation concerns the issue of convergence between Western and Chinese social policy arrangements. The point has already been made that Chinese social protection now has a greater element of marketization than does most Western provision. It has also been said that on the whole new public management themes are conspicuous by their absence in China. Yet there are certainly some elements of similarity in terms of both social policy structures and social policy outcomes. Structurally, competitive mechanisms are a common theme, whether in internal or actual markets, and their effects are not entirely dissimilar: increased commercialization, diversity, flexibility and so on. In terms of outcomes the point made repeatedly here is that inequality is on the increase in China. That too can be said about the West. The key questions would seem to be whether Chinese social policy will develop some new public management themes, and whether there will be real Western shifts towards the crude marketization seen in China. Convergence on some form of productivist social policy is certainly a possibility, but even then significant differences could remain. The safest position to take on this issue is clearly, in an echo of Mao, that it is too early to say, but the space is worth watching.

This collection, then, fills the gap in evolving debates both about reform in China and about global social policy change. It is in no sense the final word on either topic. China changes so fast that the end state is impossible to predict, as in the world beyond. Rather, it is an attempt to take analysis to the next stage by linking detailed empirical study with key comparative themes. As China travels further along the course of market reforms, the essence of its social policy reform will need to be reassessed from time to time.

China Profile (as of 1997)

1. Total Area of Territory: 9 600 000 square kilometres

2. Administrative Divisions:

   - Four municipalities directly under central administration: Beijing, Tianjin, Shanghai and Chongqing
   - Twenty two provinces: Hebei, Shanxi, Liaoning, Jilin, Heilongjiang, Jiangsu, Zhejiang, Auhui, Fujian, Jiangxi, Shandong, Henan, Hubei, Hunan, Guangdong, Hainan, Sichuan, Guizhou, Yunnan, Shaanxi, Gansu and Qinghai
   - Five autonomous regions: Inner Mongolia, Guangxi, Tibet, Ningxia and Xinjiang
   - One special administrative region: Hong Kong

3. Population:

   - Total population: 1 236 260 000
   - Sex composition: male 631 310 000 (51.07%); female 604 950 000 (48.93%)
   - Rural–urban division: urban population 369 890 000 (29.92%), rural population 866 370 000 (70.08%)
   - Birth rate: 16.57 per thousand
   - Death rate: 6.51 per thousand
   - Natural growth rate: 10.06 per thousand

4. Economy:

   - Gross National Product (GNP): 7 345 250 million yuan
   - Gross Domestic Product (GDP): 7 477 240 million yuan
   - Per capita GDP: 6079 yuan
   - GDP composition: primary industry 18.7%, secondary industry 49.2%, tertiary industry 32.1%
   - Total volume of exports: 1 515 280 million yuan
   - Total volume of imports: 1 180 580 million yuan
   - Trade balance: 334 700 million yuan

5. People's Livelihood:

   - Per capita annual net income of rural household: 2090.1 yuan
   - Per capita annual disposable income of urban household: 5160.3 yuan
   - Annual average wages of staff and workers: 6470 yuan
   - Annual per capita consumption: 2936 yuan (1930 yuan for agricultural residents and 6048 yuan for non-agricultural residents)
   - Balance of savings deposit of rural and urban residents: 4 627 980 million yuan (3762.36 yuan per capita)

6. Labour:

- Number of people employed: 696 million people
- Employment composition: primary industry 49.9%, secondary industry 23.7% and tertiary industry 26.4%; urban 202070000 (29.03%), rural 493930000 (70.97%)
- Number of urban registered unemployed: 5 700 000
- Unemployment rate: 3.1%

7. Education:

- Number of schools: 1020 regular institutions of higher education, 92 832 secondary schools, 628 840 primary schools
- Number of students enrolled: institutions of higher education 3 174 000, secondary schools 69 952 000, primary schools 139 954 000
- Number of full-time teachers: institutions of higher education 405 000, secondary schools 4 186 000, primary schools 5 794 000
- Students per teacher: institutions of higher education 7.8, secondary schools 16.7, primary schools 24.2

8. Health:

- Number of health institutions: 315 033 (67 911 hospitals)
- Number of beds: 3 135 000 (2 903 000 hospital beds)
- Number of hospital beds per 1000 population: 2.35
- Number of personnel engaged: 5 516 000 (1 985 000 doctors)
- Number of doctors per 1000 population: 1.61

9. Welfare:

- Number of social welfare institutions: 42 385
- Number of beds: 1 031 022
- Number of people housed: 785 199
- Number of social welfare enterprises: 55 509
- Total amount of social welfare and relief funds: 10 774 960 000 yuan (4 617 100 000 yuan from the government and 6 157 860 000 yuan from the collective)

10. Housing:

- Per capita floor space of residential buildings: rural areas 22.4 square metres, urban areas 8.8 square metres
- Building construction: 1286.8 million square metres under construction, 622.44 million square metres completed

11. Currency:

- 1 yuan = 0.122699 US dollar

Source: State Statistical Bureau (1998) *China Statistical Yearbook 1998*, Beijing: China Statistical Publishing House.

References

Ball, S.J. (1990). *Politics and Policy Making in Education*, London: Routledge.

Bo, X.F. and Dong, J.Z. (1993). 'Medical and Health Reforms' Difficult Manoeuvres: A Survey on Our Country's Medical and Health Reforms' (*'Yiliao weisheng gaige jubu weinan: guangyu woguo yiliao weisheng gaige de diaocha'*) (Part 1), *China's Economic Structure Reform* (*Zhongguo jingji tizhi gaige*), No. 1, pp.56–8.

Bray, M. (1996). *Counting the Full Cost: Parental and Community Financing of Education in East Asia*, Washington, DC: World Bank in collaboration with the United Nations Childrens Fund.

Buchbinder, H. and Newson, J. (1990). 'Corporate–university Linkages in Canada: Transforming a Public Institution', *Higher Education*, 20(4), pp.355–79.

Byrd, W. and Tidrick, G. (1987). 'Factor Allocation and Enterprise Incentives', in G. Tidrick and J. Chen, *China's Industrial Reforms*, Oxford: Oxford University Press.

Cai, G.X. (1997). 'Several Critical Issues to be Tackled in Guangzhou's Healthcare Reform' (*'Guangzhou yigai zhong yao jiejue de jige guanjian wenti'*), unpublished paper, Guangzhou Academy of Social Sciences.

Cai, R.H. (1997). 'Medical Insurance – Sharing the PRC Pilot Experience', paper presented at the Hospital Authority Convention on Reinventing Health Care for the 21st Century, Hong Kong Hospital Authority, 11–13 May, Hong Kong.

CCP Central Committee (1993). 'The Programme for Educational Reform and Development in China', *Zhonghua Renmin Gongheguo Guowuyuan Gongbao*, 2, pp.58–66.

Cerny, P. (1990). *The Changing Architecture of Politics: Structure, Agency and the State*, London: Sage.

Chai, C.H. (1992). 'Consumption and Living Standards in China', *The China Quarterly*, 131, pp.721–49.

Chang, Zhor Ji (1994). *Labour Market Reform in China*, Beijing: Chinese Labour Press.

Chapman, M. and Murie, A. (1996). 'Full of Eastern Promise: Understanding Housing Privatization in Post-Socialist Countries', *Review of Urban and Regional Development Studies*, 8(2), pp.156–70.

Chen, M.Z. (Minister of Health, People's Republic of China) (1997). 'China's Healthcare Reform and Development: Retrospect and Prospect' (*'Zhongguo weisheng shiye gaige yu fazhan de huigu yu zhanwang'*), Special address at the Hospital Authority Convention on Reinventing Health Care for the 21st Century, Hong Kong Hospital Authority, 11–13 May, Hong Kong.

Cheng, K.M. (1990). 'Financing Education in Mainland China: What are the Real Problems?', *Issues and Studies*, 3 (March), pp.54–75.

Cheng, K.M. (1995a). 'Education – Decentralization and the Market', in L. Wong and S. MacPherson (eds), *Social Change and Social Policy in Contemporary China*, Aldershot: Avebury.

Cheng, K.M. (1995b). '*Zhongguo Jiaoyu*' (China's Education), in X.M. Lee (ed.), *Zhongguo Shehui Fazhan* (*China's Social Development*), Hong Kong: Hong Kong Educational Publishing Company.

Cheng, K.M. (1996). 'Markets in a Socialist System: Reform of Higher Education', in K. Watson, S. Modgil and C. Modgil (eds), *Educational Dilemmas: Debate and Diversity, Vol.2 Higher Education*, London: Cassell.

Cheng, K.M. (1997). 'What have been Reformed? Review of Two Decades' Reform in China's Education', paper presented to the conference on Education and Development, Education and Geo-political Change, 11–15 September, New College, Oxford.

Cheng, T. and Selden, M. (1994). 'The Origins and Social Consequences of China's *Hukou* System', *The China Quarterly*, 139, pp.644–68.

Child, John (1994). *Management in China During the Age of Reform*, Cambridge: Cambridge University Press.

China Development Briefing, Asia Pacific Social Development Research Centre, Hong Kong, various issues.

China National Institute of Educational Research (1995). *A Study of NGO-Sponsored and Private Higher Education in China*, Beijing: Sponsored by UNESCO.

China News Analysis, 15 October, 1993.

Chiu, R. and Lupton, M. (1992). 'China's State of Flux', *Housing*, March, pp.16–17.

Choko, M.H. and Chen, Guangting (eds). (1994). *China: The Challenge of Urban Housing*, Quebec: Meridien.

Christiansen, F. (1992). ' "Market Transition" in China: The Case of the Jiangsu Labor Market, 1978–1990', *Modern China*, 18(1), pp.72–93.

Christiansen, F. (1996). 'Devolution in Chinese Higher Education Policy in the 1990s: Common Establishment and the "211" Program', *Leeds East Asia papers*, No.36.

Chu, D.K.Y. and Kwok, R.Y.W. (1990). 'China', in W. Van Vliet (ed.), *International Handbook of Housing Policies and Practices*, New York: Greenwood Press.

Dai, Guangqian (1994). 'The Establishment of an Examination and Recruitment System with Chinese Characteristics in the People's Republic of China', in J. Burns (ed.), *Asian Civil Service Systems: Improving Efficiency and Productivity*, Singapore: Times Academic Press.

Davis, D. (1988). 'Unequal Chances, Unequal Outcomes: Pension Reform and Urban Inequality', *The China Quarterly*, 114, pp.223–41.

Davis, D. (1989). 'Chinese Social Welfare: Policies and Outcomes', *The China Quarterly*, 119, pp.577–97.

Davis, D. (1992). 'Job Mobility in Post-Mao Cities', *The China Quarterly*, 132, pp.1062–85.

Davis, D. (1995). 'Inequality and Stratification in the Nineties', in C.K. Lo, S. Pepper and K.Y. Tsui (eds), *China Review 1995*, Hong Kong: Chinese University Press.

Deacon, B. (1983). *Social Policy and Socialism*, London: Pluto Press.

Deacon, B. (1993). 'Developments in Eastern European Social Policy', in C. Jones (ed.), *New Perspectives on the Welfare State in Europe*, London and New York: Routledge.

Deacon, B., Hulse, M. and Stubbs, P. (1997). *Global Social Policy: International Organizations and the Future of Welfare*, London: Sage.

Deacon, B. and Szalai, J. (eds) (1990). *Social Policy in the New Eastern Europe: What Future for Socialist Welfare?*, Aldershot: Avebury.

Deng, Xiaoping (1980). Notes of Speech to the Chinese Communist Party Leaders on 2 April 1980, quoted in *Beijing Daily*, 16 May 1984.

Dong, Richen (1994). *'Shenzhen Fanggai Liunian Huigu'* ('A Review of the Housing Reform Programme in Shenzhen in the Past Six Years'), Outline of Speech presented at the Shenzhen Housing Reform Office Seminar held on 12 September 1994 (mimeograph).

Dong, Richen (1995). *'Lengqing Hou de Chensi: Fangdichanye ji qi Fazhan'* ('Some thoughts on the fledgeling property market: the development of housing and real estate industry'), *Zhuzhai Yu Fangdichan (Housing and Real Estate)*, 16, pp.35–8.

Doyal, L. and Gough, I. (1991). *A Theory of Human Need*, London: Macmillan.

Esping-Andersen, G. (1990). *The Three Worlds of Welfare Capitalism*, Cambridge: Polity.

Feng, Lanrui (1982). *Six Questions Concerning Employment*, Beijing: Institute of Marxism-Leninism-Mao Zedong Thought, Chinese Academy of Social Sciences.

Feng, Lanrui and Zhao, Lukuan (1981). *Urban Unemployment in China*, Beijing: Institute of Marxism-Leninism-Mao Zedong Thought, Chinese Academy of Social Sciences.

Feng, T.Q. (1996). '1995–1996 *Nian: Zhongguo Zhigong Zhuangkuang de Fenxi Yu Yuce*' ('Chinese workers in 1995–1996: analysis and forecast of their situation'), in Jiang Liu, Lu Xueyi and Shan Tianlun (eds), *1995–1996 Nian Zhongguo: Shehui Xingshi Fenxi Yu Yuce (China in 1995–1996: Analysis and Forecast of the Social Situation)*, Beijing: Zhongguo Shehui Kexue Chubanshe.

Francis, Corinna-Barbara (1996). 'Reproduction of *Danwei* Institutional Features in the Context of China's Market Economy: The Case of Haidian District's High-Tech Sector', *The China Quarterly*, 147, pp.839–59.

Fu, Chonglan (ed.) (1994). *Guangzhou Chengshi Fazhan Yu Jianshe (Guangzhou City Development and Construction)*, Beijing: Zhongguo Shehui Kexue Chubanshe.

Gong, S. (1997). 'Sale of State Housing at Low Prices: Impact and Consequence', *Wuhan Real Estate*, 2 (Summer), pp.28–31.

Goodman, D.S.G. (ed.) (1997). *China's Provinces in Reform: Class, Community and Political Culture*, London: Routledge.

Goodman, R. White, G. and Kwon, H.J. (1998). *The East Asian Welfare Model*, London and New York: Routledge.

Grace, G. (1995). *School Leadership: Beyond Educational Management*, London: The Falmer Press.

Ham, C. (1997a). 'The background', in C. Ham (ed.), *Health Care Reform: Learning from International Experience*, Buckingham: Open University Press.

Ham, C. (1997b). 'Lessons and conclusions', in C. Ham (ed.), *Health Care Reform: Learning from International Experience*, Buckingham: Open University Press.

Hamer, A. (1997). 'The Linkages Between SOE Reforms, Expanding Population and Urban Housing in China', Conference paper presented to the International Symposium on Marketization of Land and Housing in Socialist China, October, Hong Kong Baptist University.

Han, Jianwei and Morishima, Motohiro (1992). 'Labor System Reform in China and its Unexpected Consequences', *Economic and Industrial Democracy*, 13(2), pp.233–61.

Hayhoe, R. (1996). *China's Universities 1985–1995: A Century of Cultural Conflict*, New York: Garland.

Henderson, G. (1990). 'Increased Inequality in Health Care', in D. Davis and E.F. Vogel (eds), *Chinese Society on the Eve of Tiananmen. The Impact of Reform*, Cambridge, MA: The Council on East Asian Studies, Harvard University.

Hills, J. (ed.) (1990). *The State of Welfare: The Welfare State in Britain Since 1974*, Oxford: Clarendon Press.

Holliday, I. (1999). 'Productivist Welfare Capitalism: Social Policy in East Asia', unpublished paper, City University of Hong Kong.

Hood, C. (1991). 'A Public Management for All Seasons?', *Public Administration*, 69, pp.3–19.

Howe, Christopher (1992). 'Foreword', in Michael Korsez, *Labour and the Failure of Reform in China*, London: Macmillan.

Hu, Tehwei *et al.* (1989). 'Household Durable Goods Ownership in Tianjin, China', *The China Quarterly*, 120, pp.786–99.

Hu, Xiaoyi (1998). '1997–1998 *Nian: Zhongguo Shehui Baoxian Zhuangkuang de Fenxi Yu Yuce*' ('1997–1998: analysis and forecast of social insurance in China'), in Ru Xin, Lu Xueyi and Shan Tianlun (eds), *1998 Nian: Zhongguo Shehui Xingshi Fenxi Yu Yuce (1998: Analysis and Forecast of the Social Situation in China)*, Beijing: Shehui Kexue Wenxian Chubanshe.

Hussain, A. (1989). 'Rural Social Security and the Economic Reforms', London: London School of Economics and Political Science.

Inkeles, Alex, Broaded, C. Montgomery and Cao, Zhongde (1997). 'Causes and Consequences of Individual Modernity in China', *The China Journal*, 37 (January), pp.31–59.

Ip, King-ming Olivia (1998). 'The Building of Labor Market in the Shenzhen Special Economic Zone and its Impact on Workplace Industrial Relations and Human Resources', unpublished PhD Thesis, University of Hong Kong, Hong Kong.

Jiaoyu Daokan, various issues.

Jing, Lin (ed.) (1996). 'Private Schools in China', *Chinese Education and Society*, 29(2), pp.1–12.

Jingji Yu Xinxi (Economy and Information), Beijing: State Planning Commission, various issues.

Johnson, N. (1990). *Restructuring the Welfare State: A Decade of Change, 1980–1990*, Hemel Hempstead: Wheatsheaf.

Jones, C. (1993), 'The Pacific challenge: Confucian welfare states', in Catherine Jones, *New Perspectives on the Welfare State in Europe*, London: Routledge, pp.198–217.

Julius, D. (1997). 'Will Chinese Universities Survive in Emerging Market Economy?', *Higher Education Management*, 9(1), pp.141–56.

Kaple, D. (1994). *Dream of a Red Factory*, New York: Oxford University Press.

Kernen, A. (1997). 'Shenyang Learns to Manage its Poor', *China Perspectives*, 11, pp.17–21.

Kornai, J. (1980). *Economics of Shortage*, Amsterdam: North-Holland.

Korzec, M. (1988). 'Contract Labor, the "Right to Work" and New Labor Laws in the People's Republic of China', *Journal of Social Policy*, 30(2), pp.117–49.

Kwong, J. (1996). 'The New Educational Mandate in China: Running Schools Running Businesses', *International Journal of Educational Development*, 16(2), pp.185–94.

Kwong, J. (1997). 'The Reemergence of Private Schools in Socialist China', *Comparative Education Review*, 41(3), pp.244–59.

Lau, Kwok Yu (1993). 'Urban Housing Reform in China Amidst Property Boom Year', in Joseph Y.S. Cheng and M. Brosseau. (eds), *China Review 1993*, Hong Kong: Chinese University Press, pp.24.1–24.35.

Lau, Kwok Yu (1997). *Housing Inequality and Segregation: An Exploratory Study on Housing Privatization in Shenzhen City of the People's Republic of China*, Working Paper Number 7, Department of Public and Social Administration, City University of Hong Kong.

Le Grand, J. and Robinson, R. (1984). *Privatization and the Welfare State*, London: Allen & Unwin.

Lee, P.N.S. (1997). 'The Provision of Occupation Benefits in Chinese Industrial Enterprises: The State, Work Unit and Society', paper presented at the International Conference on Public Sector Management Reform in China, organized by the Hong Kong Public Administration Association and Hong Kong Polytechnic University, 6–7 June, Hong Kong.

Lee, C.K. (1998). 'The Labor Politics of Market Socialism: Collective Inaction and Class Experiences Among State Workers in Guangzhou', *Modern China*, 24(1) 3–33.

Lee, C.K. (1999). 'From Organized Dependence to Disorganized Despotism: Changing Labour Regimes in Chinese Factories,' *The China Quarterly*, 157(1) 44–71.

Lee, W.O. and Li, Zibiao (1994). 'Education, Development and Regional Disparities in Guangzhou', in G.A. Postiglione and W.O. Lee (eds), *Social Change and Educational Development: Mainland China, Taiwan, and Hong Kong*, Hong Kong Centre of Asian Studies, The University of Hong Kong.

Li, Peilin (1996). '1995–1996 *Nian Guoyou Qiye Gaige de Jincheng Yu Zouxiang*' ('The process and direction of state-owned enterprise reform in 1995–1996'), in Jiang Liu, Lu Xueyi and Shan Tianlun (eds), *1995–1996 Nain Zhongguo: Shehui Xingshi Fenxi Yu Yuce (China in 1995–1996: Analysis and Forecast of the Social Situation)*, Beijing: Zhongguo Shehui Kexue Chubanshe.

Li, Shouxin and Bray, M. (1992). 'Attempting a capitalist form of financing in a socialist system: student loans in the People's Republic of China', *Higher Education*, 23, 375–87.

Li, Teiying (1997). Speech delivered in Urban Housing Reform Seminar convened by the State Council Leading Group on Urban Housing Systems Reform held on 26 December 1997, quoted in *Housing and Real Estate*, 37 (April 1998), pp.9–15.

Lieberthal K. (1995). *Governing China*, New York: Norton.

Liu, A. (1996). *Welfare Changes in China during the Economic Reforms*, Helsinki: The United Nations.

Liu, Xiaoling (1995). '*Juzhu Fenyi Xianxiang ji qi Xiangguan Yanjiu*' ('Housing segregation phenomena and related studies'), *Zhuzhai Yu Fangdichan (Housing and Real Estate)*, 19, pp.22–6.

Liu, Z.F. (1995). 'Further Reforming the Social Security System, Promoting the Introduction of Modern Enterprise System' ('*Shenhua shehui baozhang tizhi gaige, cujin xiandai qiye zhidu jianli*'), in State Economic System Reform Commission (ed.), *The Reform of the Social Security System (Shehui baozhang tizhi gaige)*, Beijing: Gaige Chubanshe.

McCormick, B.L. and Unger, J. (1996). *China after Socialism: In the Footsteps of Eastern Europe or East Asia*, New York and London: M.E. Sharpe.

Meisner, M. (1996). *The Deng Xiaoping Era*, New York: Hill & Wang.

Ming Pao, various issues.

Minzhengbu Zhengce Yanjiushi (ed.) (1986). *Minzheng Fagui Xuanbian (Selection of Civil Affairs Laws and Regulations)*, Beijing: Zhongguo Fazheng Daxue Chubanshe.

Mishra, R. (1990). *The Welfare State in Capitalist Society: Politics of Retrenchment and Maintenance in Europe, North America and Australia*, New York: Harvester Wheatsheaf.

Mok, K.-H. (1996). 'Marketization and Decentralization: Development of Education and Paradigm Shift in Social Policy', *Hong Kong Public Administration*, 5(1), pp.35–56.

Mok, K.-H. (1997a). 'Marketization and Quasi-Marketization: Educational Development in Post-Mao China', *International Review of Education*, 43(5–6), pp.1–21.

Mok, K.-H. (1997b). 'Private Challenges to Public Dominance: The Resurgence of Private Education in the Pearl River Delta', *Comparative Education*, 31(1), pp.43–60.

Mok, K.-H. (1997c). 'Professional Autonomy and Private Education in Guangdong Province', *Leeds East Asia Papers*, 41, pp.1–40.

Mok, K.-H. (1998). *Intellectuals and the State in Post-Mao China*, London: Macmillan.

Mok, K.-H. and Chan, D. (1996). 'The Emergence of Private Education in the Pearl River Delta: Implications for Social Development', in S. MacPherson and J. Cheng (eds), *Social and Economic Development in South China*, London: Edward Elgar.

Mok, K.-H. and Chan, David (1998). 'Educational Development in Guangdong in the Socialist Market Economy', paper presented to the International Teacher Education Conference, *Teacher Education in the Asia Region: Policy and Practice*, 26–30 April, East China Normal University, Shanghai, China.

Mok, K.-H. and Wat, K.Y. (1998). 'Merging of the Public and Private Boundary: Education and the Market Place in China', *International Journal of Educational Development*, 18(3), pp.255–67.

Musgrove, P. (1996). *Public and Private Roles in Health: Theory and Expenditure Patterns*, World Bank Discussion Paper 336, Washington, DC: The World Bank.

Naschold, F. (1996). *New Frontiers in Public Sector Management: Trends and Issues in State and Local Government in Europe*, Berlin: de Gruyter.

Niu, Xianmin (1997). 'The Practical Experience of the Non-governmental Nanhua Industurial and Business College', *Chinese Education and Society*, 30(1) (January–February), pp.84–9.

OECD (1995). *Governance in Transition: Public Management Reforms in OECD Countries*, Paris: OECD.

Oyen, E. (ed.) (1986). *Comparing Welfare States and their Futures*, Aldershot: Gower.

Pearson, V. (1995). *Mental Health Care in China, State Policies, Professional Services and Family Responsibilities*, London: Gaskell.

Peng, R.C. Cai, R.H. and Zhou, C.M. (1992). *Zhongguo Gaige Chuanshu: Yilao Weisheng Tizhi Gaige Juan (Medical and Health System Reform, China Reform Collection Series, 1978–91)*, Dalian: Dalian Press.

Pepper, S. (1995). 'Regaining the Initiative for Education Reform and Development', in C.K. Lo, S. Pepper and K.Y. Tsui (eds), *China Review 1995*, Hong Kong: The Chinese University Press.

Pierson, P. (1994). *Dismantling the Welfare State? Reagan, Thatcher, and the Politics of Retrenchment*, Cambridge: Cambridge University Press.

Po Yin Newsletters, various issues.

Poole, T. (1993). 'Workers Fear Loss of Rice Bowl for Life', *The Independent*, 19 March, 15.

Rosen, S. (1997). 'The Impact of Economic Reform on Chinese Education: Markets and the Growth of Differentiation', Paper presented to the Conference on Social Consequences of Chinese Economic Reform, at John K. Fairbank Center, Harvard University, 22–4 May.

Shenkar, Oded and von Glinow, Mary Ann (1994). 'Paradoxes of Organizational Theory and Research: Using the Case of China to Illustrate National Contingency', *Management Science*, 40(1), pp.56–71.

Shenzhen City Statistical Bureau (1995). *Shenzhen Tongji Shouce 1979–94* (*Shenzhen Statistical Handbook 1979–1994*).

Solinger, D. (1991). 'China's Transients and the State: a Form of Civil Society?', Hong Kong Institute of Asia Pacific Studies, Chinese University of Hong Kong.

South China Morning Post, Hong Kong, various issues.

State Education Commission (1995). *Education Law*, Beijing: State Education Commission.

Sun, G. (1992). 'Health Care Administration in China', in S.S. Nagel (ed.), *Public Policy in China*, Westport, CT: Greenwood Press. pp.53–62.

Sun, Ying (1995). '*Neidi Shehui Fuwu Tuanti Canyu Shehui Fuli Gongzuo de Lishi Jingyan, Xianzhuang Ji Pingjia*' ('Mainland social service organizations' participation in social welfare work: experiences, current situation and assessment'), in *Neidi Yu Xianggang Shehui Fuli Fazhan Di San Ci Yantaohui* (*The Third China–Hong Kong Conference on Social Welfare Development*), 7–10 November, Hong Kong.

Taylor, J.R. (1988). 'Rural Employment Trends and the Legacy of Surplus Labour, 1978–86', *The China Quarterly*, 116, pp.736–66.

Walder, Andrew (1986). *Communist Neo-Traditionalism: Work and Authority in Chinese Industry*, Berkeley, CA: University of California Press.

Wang, Ya Ping (1992). 'Private-sector Housing in Urban China 1949–1988: the Case of Xian', *Housing Studies*, 10(1), pp.57–82.

Wang, Ya Ping and Murie, Alan (1996). 'The Process of Commercialisation of Urban Housing in China', *Urban Studies*, 33(6), pp.971–89.

Wang, Ya Ping and Murie, Alan (1998). *Housing Policy and Practice in China*, London: Macmillan.

Warner, M. (1995). *The Management of Human Services in Chinese Industry*, New York: St. Martin's Press.

Wei, Feng (1996). 'The Great Tremors in China's Intellectual Circles: An Overview of Intellectuals Floundering in the Sea of Commercialism', *Chinese Education and Society*, 29(6) (November–December), pp.7–104.

Wei, Yitong and Zhang, Guocai (1995). 'A Historical Perspective on Non-Governmental Higher Education in China', Paper presented to the International Conference of Private Higher Education in Asia and the Pacific Region, November, The University of Xiamen, Xiamen.

West, A. (1995) 'Provision of public services in rural PRC', in Wong, P.W. (ed.) *Financing Local Government in the People's Republic of China*, Manila: Asian Development Bank.

West, L. (1995). 'Regional Economic Variation and Basic Education in Rural China', *Robert S. McNamara Fellowship Report*, Washington, DC: World Bank.

Westwood, R.I. and Leung, S.M. (1996). 'Work under the Reforms: The Experience and Meaning of Work in a Time of Transition', in Maurice Brosseau,

Suzanne Pepper and Tsang Shu-ki (eds), *China Review 1996*, Hong Kong: The Chinese University Press.

White, G. (1987). 'Labor Market Reform in Chinese Industry', in Malcolm Warner (ed.), *Management Reforms in China*, New York: St. Martin's Press.

White, G. (1998). 'Social Security Reform in China; towards an East Asian model?', in Goodman, White and Kwon (1998).

White, G., Murray, R. and White, C. (1983). *Revolutionary Socialist Development in the Third World*, Brighton: Wheatsheaf.

Wilding, P. (1990). 'Privatization: An Introduction and a Critique', in R. Parry (ed.), *Privatization*, London: Jessica Kingsley.

Wong, C.P.W., Heady, C. and Woo, W.T. (1996). *Fiscal Management and Economic Reform in the People's Republic of China*, Oxford: Oxford University Press (for the Asian Development Bank), Hong Kong.

Wong, L. (1994).'Privatization of social welfare in post-Mao China', *Asian Survey*, xxxiv (4), 307–25.

Wong, L. (1998). *Marginalization and Social Welfare in China*, London and New York: Routledge and LSE.

Wong, L. and Huen, Wai-po (1998). 'Reforming the Household Registration System – A Preliminary Glimpse of the Blue Chop Household Registration System in Shanghai and Shenzhen', *International Migration Review*, 32(4), pp.974–94.

Wong, L. and Lee, G. (1996). 'Welfare in Stratified Immigrant Society – Shenzhen's Social Policy Challenge', in Stewart MacPherson and Joseph Cheng (eds), *Economic and Social Development in South China*, Cheltenham: Edward Elgar.

Wong, L. and Mok, K.H. (1996). 'Dynamism and development: economic growth and social change in post-Mao China', *The Asian Journal of Public Administration*, 18(2), 2-1-33.

Wong, L. and Ngok, Kinglun (1997). 'Unemployment and Policy Responses in Mainland China', *Issues and Studies*, 33(1) (January), pp.43–63.

World Bank (1984). *Report on China*, Washington, DC: The World Bank.

World Bank (1996). *China: Pensions Systems Reform*, Report No.15121 – CHA, Beijing: Resident Mission in China (22 August).

World Bank (1997a). *China 2020. Financing Health Care: Issues and Options for China*, Washington, DC: World Bank.

World Bank (1997b) *China 2020: Old Age Security*, Washington, DC: World Bank.

Wu, G.W. (1998). 'My Joy and my Fear: People's View on Housing Reform', *Ban Yue Tan (Half-Monthly Chat)*, 7, pp.17–20.

Wu, Nianxiang (1996). '*Guangdong Sili Daixue Fazhan Chuyi*' ('A Proposal for Private University Development in Guangdong'), *Gaojiao Tansuo*, February, pp.40–4.

Wu, Ziyan (1997). '*Guangzhou Shi Jiaoyu Fazhan Zhanlue Yanjiu de Huigu jiqi Renxi*' ('Review and Study of the Strategies of the Education Development in Guangzhou'), in Wu Ziyan *et al.* (eds), *Jianshe Xiandaihua Jiaoyu Qiangshi – Guangzhoushi Jiaoyu Fazhan Zhanlue Yanjiu (Building a Strong Educational Province – Strategies of the Education Development in Guangdong)*, Guangdong: Guangdong Higher Education Press.

Xiang, Binjin and Gu, Guozhi (1996). *Zhongguo Shehui Liliang Banxue Wenti Yanjiu (Research on The Question of Social-forces Run Schools)*, Shanghai: Shanghai Shehui Kexueyuan Chubanshe.

Yao, Ruobing (1984). *Zhongguo Jiaoyu 1949–1982 (China's Education 1949–1982)*, Hong Kong: Wah Fong Bookshop Press.

Yin, Q. and White, G. (1994). 'The Marketization of Chinese Higher Education: A Critical Assessment', *Comparative Education*, 30(3), pp.217–37.

Yuan, Zhenguo and Wakabayashi, M. (1996). 'Chinese Higher Education Reform from the "State Model" to the "Social Model": Based on a Sino-Japan Comparative Perspective', *Forum of International Development Studies*, 6 (December), pp.173–200.

Yue, Songdong (1997). *Huhuan Xin de Shehui Baozhang* (Call for New Social Security), Beijing: Zhongguo Shehui Kexue Chubanshe.

Yuen, P.P. and Yan, H. (1997). 'Managed Care Systems in the People's Republic of China', paper presented at the International Conference on Public Sector Management Reform in China, organized by the Hong Kong Public Administration Association and Hong Kong Polytechnic University, 6–7 June, Hong Kong.

Zhang, Dejiang (1990). *'Jiushi Niandai Zhongguo Shehui Fuli Shiye Zhanwang'* ('Prospects of Chinese social welfare development in the 1990s'), Keynote speech given at the China and Hong Kong in the Nineties – Social Welfare Development Conference, 31 October, Beijing.

Zhang, Guixia (1996). 'Guangzhou Residential Housing Construction and Development in the Eighth Five Year Plan', *Nanfang Fangdichan* (*Southern Housing and Real Estate*), 132, pp.41–3.

Zhang, S., Fu, Y. and Lu, C.F. (1997). 'Shenzhen Real Estate Market: Present Conditions, Problems and Solutions', *Tequ Jingji* (*Special Economic Zone Economics*), 7(102), pp.44–5.

Zhang, Xing Quan (1998). *A Study of Housing Policy in Urban China*, New York: Nova Science.

Zhang, Zhaofeng (1996). 'Summary of a Symposium on Nongovernmental Basic Education', *Chinese Education and Society*, 29(5), pp.73–81.

Zhang, Zhiyi (1994). *Sili Minban Xuexiao di Lilun yu Shijian* (*Theory and Practice of Private and Minban Schools*), Beijing: Zhongguo Gongren Chubanshe.

Zheng, G.C. (1997). *The Path of Social Security with Chinese Characteristics* (*Lun Zhongguo tese de shehui baozhang daolu*), Wuhan: Wuhan University Press.

Zheng, H.R. (1987). 'An Introduction to the Labor Law of the People's Republic of China', *Harvard International Law Journal*, 28(2), pp.385–431.

Zhongguo Laodong Tongji Nianjian (*Chinese Labour Statistical Yearbook*), 1997.

Zhongguo Minzheng (*China Civil Affairs*), various years.

Zhongguo Minzheng Tongji Nianjian (*China Civil Affairs Statistical Yearbook*), various years.

Zhongguo Shehui Gongzuo (*China Social Work*), various issues.

Zhongguo Tongji Nianjian (*China Statistical Yearbook*), various years.

Zhongguo Xiangzhen Qiye Nianjian (Chinese Township and Village Enterprises Yearbook), 1997.

Zhou, C.M. (1995). *Collected Articles on Employee Medical Insurance Systems Reform* (*Zhigong yiliao baoxian zhidu gaige wenji*), Employee Medical Insurance Systems Reform Project Team, Policy and Management Research Specialists Committee, Beijing: Ministry of Health.

Zhou, Nanzhao (1989). 'Higher Education Reform in Post-Mao China 1978–1988', PhD Thesis, Buffalo University, New York.

Zhou, Nanzhao (1995). 'Strengthening the Connection between Education and Economic Development: Major Issues in China's Educational Reform and Suggested Solutions', in G. Postiglione and W.O. Lee (eds), *Social Change and*

Educational Development, Mainland China, Taiwan, and Hong Kong, Hong Kong: Centre of Asian Studies, The University of Hong Kong.

Zhou, Nanzhao *et al.* (1996). *Private Higher Education in China in the 1990s: Background, Current Status, and Research Findings,* Beijing: China National Institute of Educational Research.

Zhu, Qingfang (1998). '1997–1998 *Nian: Zhongguo Renmin Shenghuo Zhuangkuang de Fenxi Yu Yuce*' ('1997–1998: analysis and forecast of the people's living siutation in China'), in Ru Xin, Lu Xueyi and Shan Tianlun (eds), *1998 Nian: Zhongguo Shehui Xingshi Fenxi Yu Yuce* (*1998: Analysis and Forecast of the Social Situation in China*), Beijing: Shehui Kexue Wenxian Chubanshe.

Zhu, Rongji (1995). 'Zhufang gongjijin de yixie guanli wenti' (Certain management issues related to housing provident funds), speech delivered at the *National Conference on Housing Reform Experience,* 15 December 1995, Shanghai, quoted in Miao, L.Y. and Xiang, J. (1996). *Zhufang Gongjijin yu Zhufang Xindai* (Housing provident fund and housing finance), Shanghai: Zhongguo Wuzi Chubanshe, pp.136–37.

Zhu, Yiming (1996). 'Perspectives on Minban Schools in China', paper presented at the Shanghai International House for Education, 15–20 August, Shanghai.

Index